Praise for *Six Days in September*

'David Marsh, William Keegan and Richard Roberts have written a very balanced and detailed account of the events leading up to the 1992 ERM crisis. As a result of their diligent research they have unearthed many details, some which even I had forgotten. The book will be required reading for all those interested in this period.'
Lord (Norman) Lamont, Chancellor of the Exchequer (1990-93)

'As well as providing a dramatic account of the events leading to Black Wednesday, this book illustrates the stresses and strains of operating a single currency without ultimately requiring economic and eventual political union. It's an issue that's been fudged since the inception of the euro but it will never go away. It's not an argument for Brexit, but rather it should encourage consideration of a new and pragmatic settlement for Europe, one which the UK could comfortably be part of.'
Lord (Alistair) Darling, Chancellor of the Exchequer (2007-10)

'A terrific book that dissects a crucial episode in the UK's strained relationship with continental Europe and with German economic thinking.'
Prof. Harold James, Professor of History and International Affairs, Princeton University; author, Making the European Monetary Union

'*Six Days in September* is a book for those who were there at the crash of sterling out of the exchange rate mechanism. It's also for the rest of us who want to understand how the UK steadily distanced itself from European monetary union and then the European Union itself with Brexit. A riveting account written by three authors who bring their unique and varied talents to tell an electrifying story.'
Prof. Lord (Meghnad) Desai, Emeritus Professor of Economics, London School of Economics and Political Science

'A wonderful book. Living through the events before, during and after "Black Wednesday" was a dramatic experience. Reliving them through *Six Days in September* revives all the drama, but now mixed with deep insight and understanding.'
Roger Bootle, Executive Chairman, Capital Economics; author, The Trouble with Europe

'*Six Days in September* brings numerous new insights and delivers a fascinating picture of a key episode in European monetary history.'
Prof. Otmar Issing, President, Center for Financial Studies at Goethe University, Frankfurt; Board Member for Economics, Deutsche Bundesbank (1990-98) and Chief Economist European Central Bank (1998-2006)

'A hugely valuable follow-on from OMFIF's earlier splendid publication by Richard Roberts analysing the 1976 sterling crisis. Brexit is just the latest in a series of headline-grabbing, reputation-destroying British crises. While "Black" Wednesday ultimately helped Britain by (just) keeping us out of the euro, faster growth than on the continent was down to Thatcherism. Exaggerated forecasts of Brexit effects from both sides are equally implausible.'
Charles Dumas, Chief Economist, TS Lombard, formerly Lombard Street Research

'*Six Days in September* is no dry study of dreary economics. It is a dramatic story of people and politics and of events that resonate to this day.'
Sir Stephen Wall, UK Permanent Representative to the European Union (1995-2000); EU Adviser to UK Prime Minister (2000-04); author, A Stranger in Europe

'This is a brilliant book: authoritative, informative and combining the elements of a Greek tragedy with the suspense of a modern Scandinavian thriller. While stripping bare the events and personalities that led to and followed Black Wednesday, *Six Days in September* provides important insight into Britain's roller-coaster relationship with the European Union and why we are now on the verge of a catastrophic Brexit.'
Sir Brian Unwin, President, European Investment Bank (1993-2000)

'It's blood-on-the-floor stuff; who did what to whom in the finance ministries and central banks of a distinctly dysfunctional Europe. The smell of cordite is in the air.'
Andrew Hilton, Director, Centre for the Study of Financial Innovation

'An excellent book, thoroughly researched, *Six Days in September* explores the politics and economics surrounding Black Wednesday, a pivotal day for the British economy that led to the novel monetary policy regime of inflation targeting and heralded a long period of sustained growth and low inflation rates. A must-read for anyone who wants to delve into this exciting period of recent British economic history from which a lot of lessons can be drawn for the post-Brexit era.'
Prof. John (Iannis) Mourmouras, Deputy Governor, Bank of Greece; Head of Greek Prime Minister's Economic Office (2012-14)

'Keegan, Marsh and Roberts are to be congratulated on providing a first-rate account of the ERM crisis of September 1992. Parts of the story are practically unbelievable. Britain joined out of desperation at too high a rate and in secrecy without any apparent regard for the implications of German reunification. The cabinet was given an inaccurate explanation only two weeks later. At the end the pro-Europeans were still most reluctant to leave even after all our reserves were close to exhaustion. None of the protagonists emerges with any credit, save Norman Lamont. A sad warning about the pitfalls of European integration.'
Prof. Alan Sked, Professor Emeritus of International History, London School of Economics and Political Science; Founder, UK Independence Party

'This book makes for exciting reading. Black Wednesday was a dramatic event which has shaped UK attitudes to the euro and to the European Union more generally. The book underlines the contrast between the UK desire to use ERM membership primarily for the shorter-term purpose of reducing inflation, and other countries' ambition to move towards the single currency.'
Prof. Niels Thygesen, Chairman, European Fiscal Board; Emeritus Professor of Economics, Copenhagen University; Member of Delors Committee (1988-89)

Six Days
in September

Black Wednesday, Brexit
and the making of Europe

William Keegan, David Marsh
and Richard Roberts

For Christopher
with best wishes

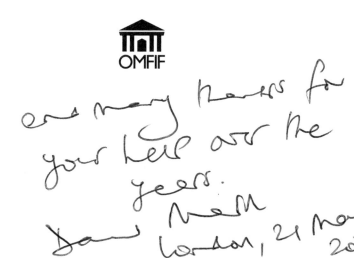
OMFIF

and many thanks for
your help over the
years.
David Marsh
London, 21 May
2018

First edition 2017

For more information about this and other OMFIF Press publications, please contact:

editorial@omfif.org
www.omfif.org

Printed by TUInk

ISBN 9780995563636

ISBN9780995563643 (e-book)

The paper used for the text pages of this book is FSC certified. FSC (The Forest Stewardship Council) is an international network to promote responsible management of the world's forests.

In memory of Sir Douglas Wass

CONTENTS

Tudo sempre acaba bem no final.
Se as coisas não estão bem, é porque você ainda não chegou ao final.

All things end well.
If they haven't, it's because they haven't yet ended.

Portuguese proverb

If François Mitterrand spoke about the D-mark being like the
Germans' nuclear weapon, this was not entirely wrong.
The Bundesbank was without doubt the dominant bank in Europe.

Hans-Dietrich Genscher

L'Europe se fera par la monnaie ou ne se fera pas.

Europe shall be made through the currency, or it shall not be made.

Jacques Rueff

Crisis and catalyst

John Nugée

In the mid-1980s, just before the Plaza agreement was signed and when the dollar was riding high, US Secretary of the Treasury Donald Regan was asked what he was going to do about the value of the dollar on international exchanges. 'There's nothing wrong with the value of the dollar,' he replied. 'It is still worth 100 cents.'

It is a long time since the British could be quite so insouciant about the international value of their currency. As long ago as the 1920s, when Winston Churchill, then chancellor of the exchequer, unilaterally returned sterling to the gold standard, and at the pre-war parity of $4.86, the international value of sterling was both crucial and controversial.

It is a theme which has since dominated the British economy. In 1949 Chancellor Hugh Dalton devalued the pound by 30% to preserve the solvency of the sterling area. Two decades after that, Prime Minister Harold Wilson's government oversaw another devaluation, this time accompanied by the memorable sound bite that 'the pound in your pocket is not worth less' – a comment which was so patently untrue that it was immediately met with the response, 'Well, not <u>totally</u> worthless.'

Sterling behaved capriciously during Margaret Thatcher's premiership – up to $2.44 in October 1980, and down almost to dollar parity in 1985 (at its lowest the pound was worth just $1.03). It was partly in response to this, and in an attempt to provide more stability, that successive chancellors first unofficially pegged sterling to the D-mark and then in 1990 made sterling a member of Europe's exchange rate mechanism.

The move was not a success. Perhaps the UK was unlucky to shackle sterling to the D-mark-dominated ERM when the D-mark itself, along with the whole German economy, was undergoing unprecedented stress and volatility following the reunification of West and East Germany. Perhaps the UK economy was not as closely aligned to continental Europe as the politicians believed. Perhaps the policy was right but the rate chosen was unwise. Whatever the cause, in under two years the pound's place in the ERM was under intolerable pressure.

This book – the second in OMFIF Press' series of 'Great British financial disasters' after Richard Roberts' earlier book, *When Britain Went Bust: The 1976 IMF Crisis* – tells the story of what came next. It is a gripping read. If it comes across like a fast-paced thriller then this is because that is precisely what it felt like at the time, with all the action concertinaed into less than a week.

There are popular villains aplenty, from the Deutsche Bundesbank, with its half-hearted defence of the ERM parities, to George Soros, the hedge fund manager profiting from others' misfortunes. There are heroes too. The Bank of England comes in for much criticism over the whole episode, but from a technical point of view its dealing desk did all that could be asked of it and more.

And there are questions; questions which even 25 years later have yet to be fully answered. Sterling's exit from the ERM was unplanned and unprecedented, and it certainly destroyed the reputation of John Major's government, a blow from which the Conservative party took nearly 20 years to recover. But it was also a catalyst for the strongest period of growth for the UK economy for many decades and quite early on, 'Black Wednesday' was being rechristened 'White Wednesday', the start of Britain's 15-year period of strength and prosperity.

And then there was the UK's June 2016 referendum on European Union membership, when the depth of the country's hostility towards the EU was laid bare. One of the new insights of this book is how this hostility can be traced all the way back to the events of 1992; how Britain's long estrangement from the EU may have been consummated in the referendum result, but owes its origins to the events of a quarter of a century earlier.

Truly, the drama of those six days in September is very much still with us today.

John Nugée is a Director of OMFIF and a former Chief Manager of Reserves at the Bank of England.

A system and its limits

Helmut Schlesinger

The monetary literature is studded with 'historic' days such as Black Friday, Black Wednesday, and so on. The importance of these landmark events may be limited to a specific country or region, or they may have overriding significance for the world economy. This book describes, with great expertise, and drawing on information from all the main sources, Britain's September 1992 departure from the exchange rate mechanism of the European Monetary System. The narrative focuses particularly on the economic and political consequences for Britain. But the indirect effects extend far wider. The authors see in the 1992 developments the beginning of the UK's separation from European Union membership, due to take effect in March 2019.

The events described in *Six Days in September* make clear how, right from the start, there were different judgements of the political value of Britain's EMS entry. One important consideration was that membership of the ERM would contribute to damping Britain's strong inflationary tendencies. Many countries which entered the system of fixed exchange rates with relatively narrow bands, however, underestimated the system's weaknesses, particularly its vulnerability to speculative attacks. A speculator acting on the expectation of a member country's devaluation could expect high profits in the event that a devaluation took place, but practically no risk if it didn't.

The weaknesses of a fixed rate system are already apparent when a currency enters it. Corrections of entry rates (through realignments) proved necessary for quite a few currencies both after the formation of the European currency 'snake' and following the start of the ERM in 1979. Several experts believed the pound's ERM entry rate in 1990 was too high – but a thorough, open discussion about this among the partner countries did not take place. The market's assessment of the pound, and the pressure on the exchange rate towards the lower intervention rate, pointed in the same direction. One form of defence – often with only a limited impact – consists of changing interest rate differentials between the 'weak' and the 'strong' currency. Specific problems in individual partner countries worked against this method. Inevitably there were loud calls for the Bundesbank to lower interest rates. But the German economy was in a historically unique situation. The politically justified, rapid unification of the two differently structured parts of Germany had led to strong monetary tensions, especially accelerating inflation. The Bundesbank had to fight this with high interest rates. On the other hand, the economic situation in some countries in the EMS demanded an interest rate reduction.

To resolve such tensions, the rules of the monetary system allowed for the possibility of exchange rate adjustments. Under the fixed rate Bretton Woods system, in force up to 1973, Germany had learned the difficulties of carrying out such parity changes within one's own country. In the days leading up to Black Wednesday, with the Bundesbank forced into obligatory intervention on a daily basis to support individual currencies, especially the Italian lira, it asked the German government to pave the way for an ERM realignment. The federal government assigned to this task the two deputies of the finance minister and the Bundesbank president. The partial success of their mission to Rome should, according to the ERM rules, have led to a meeting of the European Monetary Committee. Instead, the committee chairman replaced a summit with bilateral telephone conversations. Later information has shown that Britain did not know about the German initiative. So, initially, nothing happened apart from the devaluation of the Italian lira.

Thus, as described in this book, speculation escalated towards the devaluation of more currencies; the Spanish peseta and Portuguese escudo soon changed their parities. For sterling, the tension was defused only with the British government's decision to leave the ERM. I regret to this day – without being able to assess the effect – that a general remark by myself, not focused especially on the pound, should have played a role in aggravating sterling's position. In fact, George Soros, the most powerful speculator at the time, had already geared himself to the pound's depreciation.

The ERM system with narrow bands for exchange rate fluctuations among the partner countries failed because of its own over-ambitious construction. This became clear when the franc came under pressure with the next major upheaval in the system, in summer 1993. At that time, on Germany's request, it was decided to widen the bands, and on France's request, a range was set of plus-minus 15%. This eliminated the incentive for risk-free speculation on parity changes and the ERM functioned without tensions until the introduction of the euro in 1999.

This book's impressive review of the period shows the depth of British political clashes linked to Black Wednesday. In every country government decisions on exchange rates changes have led to disputes not only between parties, but also within them. In the case of the UK, however, another factor played a role: the decision to reject the devaluation foreseen under ERM rules, and leave the EMS, reversed the loss of national autonomy associated with membership of the system. The long-standing member countries of the European Community had on the other hand gathered experience over nearly 50 years which, in many respects, limited their political freedom of action. These were constraints to which they had themselves agreed, with full regard for their decision-making freedom. Since the creation of EMU, these limitations have become still more pronounced in the field of money than in most other areas of economic and social life.

The 1999 transition to the single currency abolished the exchange rate for economic interactions among member countries. But the euro by no means eliminated economic tensions. Divergences were again exacerbated in individual countries' economic development after the outbreak of the 2008 financial crisis. As exchange rate changes were no longer available as a means of adjustment, imbalances had to be reduced with the aid of financial and monetary policy instruments. These measures promoting internal adjustment generated some severe domestic political tensions in the countries concerned, as well as sporadic turbulence in relationships between member states. Despite this, these countries and ultimately their citizens appear to be in an advanced state of integration. And the practical difficulties now facing Britain's exit from the union offer other member states little encouragement to follow the same path.

Prof. Helmut Schlesinger was President of the Deutsche Bundesbank in 1991-93 and Deputy President in 1980-91.

AUTHORS' NOTE

A tale of skirmishes

Upon embarking on this book, we were occasionally asked, 'What are you working on now?' When we said, 'A book on the 25th anniversary of Black Wednesday,' most younger people would say they had never heard of Black Wednesday. Those who had, or were around at the time, tended to ask, 'Is it really 25 years?' Then there were others who, understandably, confused it with some of the stock market crashes of recent decades. It was surprising how many remember it as the time when UK interest rates shot up to 15% – because they never did. That turned out to be an empty threat. The interest rate rise announced at the nadir of sterling's fortunes on 16 September was rescinded as soon as Britain announced it was leaving the European exchange rate mechanism. We must not forget those in the City of London at the time who said they were about to uncork the champagne, on the grounds that 15% interest rates would bankrupt them and they might as well go down fighting. The ERM adventure, and the nature of the exit, undoubtedly added an important ingredient to the poison which infected Britain's relationship with the rest of Europe – a poison that tipped the scales in the 2016 referendum decision to leave the European Union.

Four successive Conservative prime ministers – Margaret Thatcher, John Major, David Cameron and Theresa May – have encountered terminal or near terminal problems over Europe. The same fateful issue has bedevilled their chancellors of the exchequer, the men (the UK has had two female prime ministers, but never a female chancellor) normally reckoned to hold the second-most important Cabinet job – Geoffrey Howe, Nigel Lawson, Major himself (under Thatcher), Norman Lamont and Kenneth Clarke among them. For the Conservatives, the schism over Europe has been the political equivalent of Germany's 17th century 30-years war – a convoluted and deadly series of encounters between Protestant and Catholic states in the fragmented Holy Roman Empire, escalating into a wider conflict that drew in most of the great European powers. One of Thatcher's problems in the 1980s was that, within her Cabinet, she was outnumbered by pro-European colleagues. The constellation changed after Black Wednesday, which strengthened Eurosceptic forces. Major's prime ministership was blighted by sniping over Europe from rebellious fellow Conservatives he famously termed 'the bastards'. The political fallout nullified any positive effect from the UK's impressive post-1992 economic recovery. Conservative skirmishes over Europe, in different permutations, have rumbled on ever since.

The ERM debacle, like the 30-years war, had ramifications beyond national borders. Black Wednesday was an earthquake in Britain, but the tremors made themselves felt in many other countries. The underlying reason for the misadventure was the sheer incompatibility of German economic and monetary policies in the boom years immediately following Germany's reunification with those required in other European countries, which were suffering recession-like conditions. In 1990 and 1991 Germany's real GDP rose 5% per year, compared with stagnating or contracting economies in the UK and elsewhere in Europe.

Against a background of near-total non-convergence with the strongest economy in Europe, the self-confidence with which Britain fixed and then tried to maintain a relatively demanding exchange rate against the D-mark within the ERM is close to breathtaking. Some observers – George Soros, the fund manager and philanthropist, was one of them – spotted the disconnect. Marking the first time hedge funds had intervened to determine the outcome of a major exchange rate upheaval, Britain's 1992 debacle served as a dress rehearsal for the Asian financial crisis five years later.

The currencies of many southeast Asian economies, pegged to the dollar with insufficient flexibility for adjustment, came under widespread attack in 1997-98, including at the hands of the same hedge funds that had featured in 1992. The spark came from free-flowing international capital flows (sometimes mobilised simply to avoid losses or preserve investors' or companies' capital rather than to make profits). The root cause was the same as in 1992: misaligned exchange rates, confronting countries with the task of amending monetary conditions for international reasons in a way that contradicted domestic economic and political requirements.

The perturbations of 1992, although they appeared at the time to strengthen the Deutsche Bundesbank and slow the momentum to economic and monetary union, ended up having precisely the opposite effect – but with longer-term implications that gravely undermined the institutional base of EMU and, in the aftermath of the 2008-09 financial crisis, almost caused its downfall.

The reality was threefold. First, the Bundesbank, having ascended to the pinnacle of its power, was weakened as Germany faced up to the negative economic repercussions of the widespread exchange rate realignments of 1992-93. The sharp revaluation of the D-mark held back exports, depressed growth and severely hampered Germany's own task of meeting the Maastricht criteria for budgetary rectitude. Second, because Europe's politicians saw the ERM's all-too-evident vulnerability, they implicitly recognised the validity of the criticism of Alan Walters, Thatcher's economic adviser, that the ERM was 'half-baked', being neither a fully-fledged single currency nor a fixed-rate system assisted by capital controls. As a result, Europe collectively took a decision – with which Sir Alan would not have concurred – to proceed as speedily as possible towards the single currency nirvana, supposedly to eliminate the risk that anything like Black Wednesday would ever happen again. Third, the ebbing of Bundesbank authority, German reluctance to impose a roadblock to EMU and general Franco-German incoherence in the 1990s over formulating effective EMU rules heightened the euro area's eventual vulnerability to crisis.

As a result of all these factors flowing directly and indirectly from Black Wednesday, monetary union started under a false dawn. With perpetual fixing of exchange rates, currency crises were thought to be banished to the history books. Governments believed they could rely on individual countries' payments surpluses and deficits being automatically financed at a constant exchange rate through the balancing mechanism of euro capital flows. Europe's complacency was bolstered rather than punctured by the imbalances built up in another fixed exchange rate system in the 1990s, this time in Asia – affecting a series of countries to different degrees, including South Korea, Hong Kong, Indonesia, Malaysia, the Philippines and Thailand. This led to sizeable devaluations in 1997-98 as countries were forced to depart from their dollar peg, requiring massive volumes of emergency lending and draconian conditions from the International

Monetary Fund. These conditions stored up considerable political acrimony which left a mark well into the 21st century. This explains why many Asian countries were reluctant to turn ever again to the Fund for financing needs, and preferred to build up their reserves to stave off possible balance of payments problems.

These issues were not immediately apparent to the Europeans. Had finance ministries and chancelleries in Europe been more attuned to learning from mistakes made elsewhere, the Asian crisis might have served as a warning signal. The current account imbalances built up in the euro area were roughly twice as large – and continued for twice as long – as those in the Asian currency bloc in the 1990s. Both these imbalances and the flows of short-term capital that financed them were unsustainable. However, in the belief that members of a monetary union would be immune from unpleasant consequences, the Europeans failed to heed the cautionary tale.

Could it have turned out differently? Undoubtedly, the answer is Yes. One of the reasons for writing this book was the authors' rather naive view that someone, somewhere might indeed learn from what John Major has called, in a Majoresque word, a 'concatenation' of extraordinary circumstances. Less politely, but more prosaically, the sheer scale of the tragicomic bungling that we chronicle in the months and weeks leading up to and away from Black Wednesday adds up to a rattling good yarn. As in all collaborative actions where three authors try to draw a common thread through a complex tale, we have relied on quantities of patience and endurance to assemble and knead together the necessary material.

We carried out the project in roughly five months, relying on a mixture of contemporary and past accounts as well as our own diverse experience. Scores of players in the drama too numerous to list here – a number of whom have regrettably died in recent years – have helped us over the decades to piece together what we all believe is a remarkable narrative. We would like to display our gratitude in particular to Helmut Schlesinger, former president of the Bundesbank, who features prominently in the narrative, for writing a thought-provoking foreword. We would like to thank archival and policy staff from various public institutions – singling out, among others, Jan Booth, Monica Murariu and Monica Wilson at the Treasury, Michael Anson at the Bank of England, Mark Dunton at the UK

National Archives and Michael Best and Martin Roesch at the Bundesbank – for their assistance.

Our main thanks are due to the indefatigable colleagues at OMFIF who have once again excelled themselves in producing and marketing a book in record time. We are grateful to William Coningsby-Brown, Julian Frazer, Simon Hadley, Catherine Lockwood and Angela Willcox on the production side as well as to Sarah Butler, Sarah Holmes, Stella Emseis, Liz Goopy, Danae Kyriakopoulou, Edward Longhurst-Pierce, Derval O'Neill, Sam Nugée, Bhavin Patel and Marcin Stepan.

Even after the appearance of large numbers of books and articles on this subject, research is work in progress. The various public bodies have yet to release many of the most revealing archival files from 1990-92, although they have made a start under the modified 30-year rule, and some disclosures have been made under Freedom of Information procedures. This will not be the last book on Black Wednesday.

Prologue

CHAPTER ONE

'Tool that broke in my hands'

At 7.30pm on Wednesday 16 September 1992 Norman Lamont, chancellor of the exchequer, stepped into the British Treasury's neoclassical courtyard in the heart of Whitehall. A blaze of flash-guns turned dusk to day. He delivered in measured tones a terse 138-word statement to the battery of reporters, photographers and TV cameras from around the world. 'Today has been an extremely difficult and turbulent day,' Lamont intoned. 'Massive speculative flows continued to disrupt the functioning of the exchange rate mechanism.'

The message was that Britain was suspending membership of the ERM, the arrangement that linked the currencies of participating European Community members in the European Monetary System, and cancelling an emergency rise in Britain's interest rate to 15% announced earlier that afternoon.

During a hectic spell of intervention on the markets, the Bank of England's dealers had been selling dollars, D-marks and other currencies to buy enormous sums of sterling offered from all over the world at the lowest permitted level within the ERM, DM2.778. The combined selling had drained the nation's foreign exchange reserves.

For Lamont, an agnostic on the ERM who had taken over as chancellor when John Major succeeded Margaret Thatcher as prime minister in November 1990, this was a cataclysm that blighted the rest of his parliamentary career. 'The market has won,' proclaimed a headline the next day. 'Sell, sell, sell again – a diary of disaster,' ran another. 'Beaten Lamont devalues pound,' yet another, and 'Honey, I shrunk the £.'

Just a few hours earlier at 4pm, two miles eastward in the heart of the City of London, Ian Plenderleith, the Bank of England's assistant director in charge of markets, made a less public announcement that also marked the denouement of an extraordinary day. Plenderleith, when not participating in frantic crisis management with opposite numbers in Whitehall, had been moving back and forward into the Bank's dealing room to assess the state of the battle against speculators. It was an unequal struggle.

The foreign exchange market was conducted largely by telephone between the big commercial banks. The Bank of England maintained a continual presence in the market and had an obligation under ERM rules to buy reactively as much sterling offered to it at its 'intervention rate', which was the bottom of its ERM band. As long as the price of sterling was above its ERM floor, there were few buyers.

When the avalanche of intervention ended at 4pm – the cut-off time when the obligation in the ERM rules for central banks to maintain their exchange rate within the official currency band ceased for the day – the pound dropped through its ERM floor. Plenderleith strode into the room to give the dealers a morale-rallying address. The compact trading team of eight dealers was exhausted after a uniquely busy day. Before them lay the thankless task of manually reconciling the large number of individual trades to ensure buyers and sellers were paid out at the correct level. During the process the Bank would discover the exact size of the accounting loss during the day – a figure that the Treasury later put (with considerable caveats as to the manner of calculation) at £3.3bn.[1]

In the aftermath, Treasury officials were at pains to play down to their political masters the exact extent of the fall in reserves to negative levels.

In the manner of a commanding officer addressing his troops, Plenderleith thanked the dealers for their efforts. He told them, whatever their understandable qualms about the size of intervention and the losses that had ensued, that they had acquitted themselves well in carrying out Bank operations. 'This has been a bad day for Britain, but you have fully lived up to your responsibilities as professional central bankers.'[2]

The pronouncements from the pair of British institutions most deeply involved in the tumult brought the curtain down on a two-year adventure that started when the UK joined the ERM, on a tide of euphoria, in October 1990. The climax had been building up in financial markets over a six-day period starting on Friday 11 September. The saga made profits running into billions of dollars for international speculators and banks.

Mark Clarke of Bank of America – who went public afterwards on his £10m Black Wednesday windfall – recalled the moment when it happened:

> At four o'clock suddenly the Bank of England wasn't supporting pounds. Instead of a load of noise coming out of the voice brokers and everything and around the dealing room, everyone sat in stunned silence, for almost two or three seconds, and all of a sudden it erupted, and sterling just free-fell. That sense of awe, that the markets could take on a central bank and actually win. I couldn't believe it...[3]

The foreign exchange unrest was closely linked to nervousness about a probable knife-edge result in a referendum in France the following Sunday 20 September to decide on French approval of the Maastricht treaty, aiming to integrate Europe with a single currency – a controversial project not just in the UK, but across much of Europe. The acute phase had begun the previous day in Frankfurt. On the afternoon of Tuesday 15 September Helmut Schlesinger, president of the Bundesbank, Germany's resolutely independent central bank, had given an ill-fated interview to two reporters from *Handelsblatt* and the *Wall Street Journal*, the German and US business newspapers.

Schlesinger, a courteous and meticulous 68-year-old economist who had spent most of his working life at the Bundesbank, had taken over the top position the previous year on the resignation of Karl Otto Pöhl, his mercurial and much better-known predecessor. Schlesinger could carry out every job in the economics and statistics department of the Bundesbank, but was unschooled in dealing with the media. The subject matter – a botched attempt the previous weekend to realign exchange rates to release some of the strains that were building up in the ERM pressure cooker – was toxic. The changes in parities were only modest, specifically a devaluation of the Italian lira, which had fallen through its ERM floor the previous Friday.

Britain decided it wanted no part of the realignment: sterling could stand strong on its own. The Bundesbank accompanied the currency change with a grudging cut in German interest rates on Monday. The prevailing opinion in financial markets was that the parity adjustment did not go far enough to ease tensions. More importantly, Schlesinger, in the fateful Tuesday interview, said so too.

An 'unauthorised' version of his comments, sent by *Handelsblatt* to news agencies on Tuesday evening, stated Schlesinger's belief that further ERM pressure was probable before 20 September. The news caught the UK authorities wrong-footed. As Andrew Turnbull, head of the Treasury's monetary department at the time, commented, the British government was making contingency plans for an upsurge of speculation after the 20 September French referendum, but not for five days earlier on Tuesday evening. 'We were caught out by Schlesinger's remarks.'[4]

The Bundesbank revelations prompted a volley of sell orders from around the world, especially New York, where trading was in full swing. In London, British ministers and officials reacted with fury. At a US embassy dinner party on Tuesday evening, Lamont gave full vent to his feelings. Another guest, Richard Lambert, editor of the *Financial Times*, recalled, 'Norman Lamont arrived late and kept popping out of the room. Lamont came up to me, somewhat agitated, and said, "The *FT* is running a story that you know to be a lie, which will have awful consequences." I got on the telephone to the office, and found out that the Schlesinger statement was the front page story.'[5]

From the dinner Lamont ordered further Bank of England efforts to seek Bundesbank clarification. As Robin Leigh-Pemberton, the patrician governor of the Bank of England, said later, 'Norman Lamont rang up from his dinner to ask me to get on the phone to Schlesinger, to ask him to retract what he had said. I was quite agreeably surprised that I was able to get through to Schlesinger at his home. He said he was trying to sort it out. His attitude was rather apologetic. It was along the lines of: "I'm terribly sorry, Robin, oh dear, I never thought of that."'[6]

One of the more rocambolesque reasons for the communications misadventures – in the days before widespread use of mobile phones – was the absence from the scene of Manfred Körber. The normally assiduous head of the Bundesbank press office (who later took on the same job at the European Central Bank) was out of telephone contact in a restaurant celebrating his birthday west of Frankfurt on Tuesday evening.

Major commented afterwards, 'I believe this was incompetence and clumsiness rather than malice. Had it not been for the Schlesinger statement, I think we would have survived the week. If you have the governor of the second most important central bank in the world pointing markets in a certain direction, markets will follow that lead.'[7] Terry Burns, the Treasury's permanent secretary during the ERM crisis, took a similar view. Burns believes the Bank of England should have been more effective in communicating with its opposite numbers at the Bundesbank during the ERM experience. But he says the Schlesinger episode reflected 'more cock-up than conspiracy'. Schlesinger, with whom he had had an amiable relationship at international policy meetings such as at the Organisation for Economic Co-operation and Development in Paris, 'was not a man to engage in conspiracies – it's not in his nature.'[8]

Whatever the motivation, the Bundesbank remarks had a lethal effect on sterling. In New York, where trading was in full swing, Schlesinger's 'disastrous' comments triggered a sell-off of sterling to below its ERM floor.[9] This presented traders with an opportunity to make an easy profit since the Bank of England was obliged under ERM rules to buy sterling offered to it at its intervention rate of DM2.778 during London trading hours. By the close of trading in New York, a substantial volume of sterling had been bought for presentation at the Bank the next day.

The debacle went on uninterrupted the whole of the following day. One reason Major and his ministers did not suspend sterling's participation earlier in the day reflected their wish to consult formally with European partners and fulfil the strict procedures for departure, in case the UK decided to rejoin the scheme – a vision that turned out to be wholly illusory.

Another factor was the fear that suspension in the middle of the trading day would have left commercial banks around the world with uncovered trading positions that the Bank would not have honoured when the market closed at 4pm. This could have caused large losses and even a banking crisis.

Amid the fallout from the currency debacle, James Callaghan, a veteran of past sterling crises – he had been Labour chancellor of the exchequer under Harold Wilson at the time of the 1967 devaluation, and prime minister during the 1976 International Monetary Fund crisis – observed with Delphic foreboding, 'The skies are darkening with the wings of chickens coming home to roost.'[10]

But for Lamont the skies were clearing: 'We are floating and we will set monetary policy in this country to meet our objectives,' he told a

BBC interviewer on Friday 18 September. 'It will be a British monetary policy.'[11] Black Wednesday – or White Wednesday, as it was dubbed by commentators like Anatole Kaletsky, economics editor at *The Times*, who saw the withdrawal as a liberation from deflationary forces[12] – generated some surprisingly mixed results. The day of disruption was a day of paradox. The Bundesbank appeared the victor of the skirmish. But September 1992, together with the almost equally serious exchange rate upsets the following year centred on the French franc, gave further impetus to European monetary union, in which the German central bank lost most of its power.

The 1992-93 upheavals helped persuade Schlesinger that there was little alternative to a full-scale merger of hitherto separate currencies in Europe, because of the political impossibility of making timely realignments in a system of fixed but adjustable rates. This was a notable conversion. Schlesinger and other old-school Bundesbank policy-makers had been among the most important sceptics about monetary union. After 1992-93, as he explained later, the tide changed.

> The exchange rate crises of 1992 and 1993 gave rise to a great deal of emotion and were highly politicised. One example was the way that English newspapers wrote about the Bundesbank and portrayed Hitler standing in front of the Bundesbank building. It was extremely difficult, if not impossible, to bring about realignments that would have been sensible for economic reasons. The problem of the EMS was that it was no longer a risk, but an encouragement, for speculators. I realised there was no option but to proceed directly to monetary union for the countries that were ready for it.[13]

The Bundesbank was both villain and hero. At the height of the debacle, British government officials briefed the press that sterling had been laid low by persistent Bundesbank sniping. This had been the fifth time within weeks that the Bundesbank tried to sabotage sterling's membership of the currency scheme, according to British officials quoted by the *Financial Times*.[14]

An alternative view was put forward by William Keegan in *The Observer*. When the UK joined the ERM in October 1990, he declared that the chosen rate was too high. This qualified him, according to Major in his memoirs, 'as one of the few commentators deserving to speak not simply with hindsight about the ERM experience.'[15] Keegan wrote on 20 September:

> The accusation is that the joint Major-Lamont strategy of not taking 'the soft option' and devaluing the pound was torpedoed by the injudicious, nay, actively malicious remarks by the Bundesbank. The markets noted that the Bundesbank wanted a realignment; the pressure on the pound became uncontainable; and our valiant heroes fell gamely to the Hun. What utter nonsense! The truth is that, if the Bundesbank did play a key role in the collapse of the government's economic strategy, it has done this country a great service. Instead of being pilloried by a tetchy British prime minister, Dr Helmut Schlesinger, president of the Bundesbank, should be given a knighthood... It was not just the Germans who thought the situation unsustainable. After the searing experience the central banks had had in failing to defend the lira the previous week, senior British officials knew early last week that the devaluation of sterling was only a matter of time. Prominent among the Bundesbank's critics have been the people who, until last week, argued that we in Britain should be best served by handing the reins of economic power over to the solid and reliable Bundesbank. But when that venerable institution takes a view about policy, its erstwhile champions do not like it. This should come as no surprise to serious students of British consistency.[16]

The Bank of England, in contrast to the Bundesbank, gained from the episode. The end of the ERM experiment ushered a new period in British monetary policy in which the government allowed the central bank autonomy in setting interest rates to meet inflation targets – a step that successive governments had been highly reluctant to take in view of the widespread opinion in British politics that interest rate decisions were too important to leave to unelected technocrats. The post-Black Wednesday measures culminated in the Bank being given operational independence in monetary policy when the Labour government took office in 1997. And this coincided with an above-average period of British economic growth that extended well into the 21st century, including in the years immediately after the 2008-09 financial crisis.

Jacques de Larosière, the urbane governor of the Banque de France at the time of the 1992 upheavals, previously managing director of the IMF and later president of the European Bank for Reconstruction and Development, gave a typically forensic summary:

> The departure of sterling on 16 September – the famous Black Wednesday – was particularly traumatic and sealed Britain's future of upholding of monetary independence. Chancellor Lamont, who had honestly played the card of European monetary co-operation, suffered a harsh and humiliating experience (reserves down $28bn in one day!). Mr Schlesinger, president of the Bundesbank, contributed to unleashing the wave of speculation with an affirmation, which turned out to be imprudent, of the need, in his view, to proceed with a bigger realignment, including sterling, than the one limited to the lira.[17]

Lamont, somewhat unfairly given his initial scepticism about joining the ERM in 1990, had to endure massive political opprobrium from the setback. Yet he later drew some relatively sanguine conclusions. With the launch of the euro at the beginning of 1999, the Bundesbank lost its power. Conversely, 'in so far as it precipitated Britain's departure from the ERM, the Bundesbank helped put the Bank of England on the path to independence and to becoming a Bundesbank for Britain,' benefiting from a financial framework 'for its own conditions'.[18] The overall outcome from ERM membership was 'not unsatisfactory' given the rapid fall in inflation during the two years. 'Just as the policy was becoming too severe, the markets intervened, and Britain was able to resume growth, unlike its continental neighbours. The ERM was a tool that broke in my hands when it had accomplished all that it could usefully do.'[19] Unhelpfully for Lamont and his boss John Major, it was also a tool that broke the back of the British government.

CHAPTER TWO

When George Soros won

'It was an absolute avalanche of speculation,' said an awestruck Bank of England official in the thick of the pressure on sterling. 'There had been nothing like it before.'[1] The key new factor was hedge funds. These aim to maximise profits on trading operations by borrowing stocks or currencies to generate 'leverage' through short-selling instruments likely to fall in value. They played no part in the 1971-73 breakdown of the Bretton Woods fixed exchange rate system or in the sterling crises of 1967 and 1976. There had been plenty of selling of dollars and pounds in those episodes by holders anxious to pre-empt the depreciation of their assets from devaluation, but not of hedge fund short-selling to generate profits. Sterling's 1992 ERM crisis marked the public arrival of hedge funds as a powerful force on the international monetary scene.

The first hedge fund was established in 1949 in New York by Alfred Winslow Jones, an eclectic investor who started his firm A.W. Jones & Co. at the age of 48 after earlier spells at the Berlin foreign ministry, as an observer for the Quakers in the Spanish Civil War, and an editor for the US magazine *Fortune*. Over the next 20 years Jones' fund made a cumulative return of almost 5,000%; an investment of $10,000 in 1949 was worth $480,000 by 1968.[2] Jones focused on US stocks and brought together three key elements: a private company, thus avoiding restrictive banking and securities regulations; short-selling, in addition to long positions, to reduce market risk; and leverage, to maximise returns.[3] The term 'hedge fund' first appeared in an article about Jones and his business model in *Fortune* in 1966. Financial journalist Carol Loomis highlighted the outperformance of Jones' funds compared to best-performing mutual funds and dubbed him 'one of the wonders of Wall Street'.[4]

Jones' success led to imitators. A Securities and Exchange Commission study of 1968 identified 140 hedge funds with assets of $2bn, many of them recent creations inspired by Loomis' article. But the bear market of the early 1970s resulted in investor withdrawals of funds. A further SEC study estimated assets in 1971 were down to $1bn. The 1970s and early 1980s were difficult times for the industry, which reached 'rock bottom' in 1984, by which time hedge fund numbers had fallen to just 68.[5]

The mid-1980s saw the start of a second cycle of hedge fund development, with rapid and continuous expansion. Between 1988 and the peak in 2007, the number of US hedge funds grew to 13,000 from 1,000 while the value of assets rose to $2.3tn from around $200bn. Most of the early second-generation hedge funds were 'macro' funds featuring an opportunistic approach based on macroeconomic variables and taking positions in relation to currencies, interest rates, inflation and fiscal policy as well as stocks. In 1990 macro funds comprised 70% of industry assets, though the proportion subsequently declined with the advent of additional strategies. The industry was decidedly asymmetrical, with a few large and relatively long-standing fund groups and many smaller and often short-lived funds.

The 1980s and 1990s witnessed the rise of Soros Fund Management. It was founded by George Soros, a Hungarian-born graduate of the London School of Economics who had studied under philosopher Karl Popper. Having worked in a variety of jobs, including as a railway porter, waiter, and fancy goods salesman in Welsh seaside souvenir shops, Soros broke into the finance industry in the 1950s and set up his own fund in 1973, subsequently renamed the Quantum Fund in 1978. By then its assets had grown 100-fold to near $400m and Soros had amassed a personal fortune of $100m. In 1981 *Institutional Investor* hailed him as 'the world's greatest money manager'.[6] Distracted by other pursuits, including his interest in philosophy and philanthropy, Soros neglected the fund and that year Quantum incurred its first loss.

Upon his return to full-time investment in 1984, Soros adopted a broader macro focus as fitting the rapidly globalising international economy. 'He will invest anywhere in the world, in spot or futures markets, in shares, bonds, currencies, commodities and gold,' observed *The Economist*. 'He is, in a sense, the ultimate speculator.'[7] In 1985 he focused particularly on the dollar, which since 1980 had appreciated by around 50% against other major currencies, contributing to the gaping US current account deficit and mounting protests by US industry. By August Soros was convinced the reversal point was near and waded into the market, buying $720m of the currencies likely to rise against the dollar, an exposure 10 times larger than Quantum's capital. Initially the bet went badly as the dollar continued to rise and soon the position was $20m down. But on 22 September the finance ministers of the five leading economies signed the Plaza agreement (named after the New York hotel in which it was concluded), laying a framework for coordinated intervention to depress the dollar; Soros made an overnight profit of $30m. But instead of banking his winnings, he doubled up. The dollar continued to fall and by the time he realised his gains Quantum was up $230m, its first great currency coup.

Soros' book *The Alchemy of Finance*, published in May 1987, related his investment experience with the dollar and reinforced his status as a celebrity. Another outcome was a meeting with Stanley Druckenmiller, a rising star among Wall Street mutual fund managers who was keen to meet the legendary investor. They got on well and Soros offered him the job of running Quantum. Druckenmiller initially declined but Soros persisted and he eventually joined Soros Fund Management as manager of the Quantum Fund in late 1988. Druckenmiller, like Soros, had begun his career focused on stock exchange investment. But he also had a good grasp of currencies and interest rates derived from macroeconomics and an unfinished economics PhD. Druckenmiller, observed a colleague, understood the stock market better than economists and understood economics better than stock pickers.[8] In addition to his grasp of fundamentals, Druckenmiller was strong in technical and chart analysis of the markets and trading. It was a formidable skill set.

Soros moved to London in 1989; the fall of the Berlin Wall in November promised wider scope for the development of his philanthropic interests in eastern Europe. Although in semi-retirement, Soros continued to take a close interest in the business, of which he was the biggest owner, and himself managed a couple of relatively smaller funds. For Druckenmiller, the market turbulence and tensions generated by German unification in 1990 and the disintegration of the Soviet empire provided extraordinary opportunities for traders with a good macroeconomic grasp. In the five years from 1989 to 1993 he delivered returns of more than 50% per year and Quantum's assets soared to $5bn from $1.8bn, while Soros Fund Management's total assets grew to $8.3bn. Best of all was the result in 1992, the year of sterling's ERM exit.

Soros and Druckenmiller were alert to the potential explosive dimensions of the European dilemma. Soros had already gained insights into the Bundesbank's philosophy and tactics, partly through having observed Schlesinger's view on sterling at an investment conference in Frankfurt a few weeks before the September upheaval. The Bundesbank was responding to inflation generated by German unification with a series of interest rate rises. But other European countries linked to the D-mark via the ERM were in recession and needed credit loosening, not tightening. The interest rate differentials caused funds to flow into a strengthening German currency, while the lira and the pound were moving towards the bottom of their ERM bands and threatened to dip below.

In the summer of 1992 Druckenmiller concluded that these circumstances were unsustainable. Either Germany had to cut its rates, which was unlikely, or Britain had to raise its rate or drop out of the ERM. British mortgages were floating-rate, so a rate rise would immediately translate into higher loan payments. This would be very painful for homeowners and hit demand in an economy that was already mired in recession. Druckenmiller perceived that, for a hedge fund, there was little downside and considerable possible upside. The pound was highly unlikely to rise against the D-mark, but there was a significant possibility that Britain would relieve the pressure by devaluation through quitting the ERM. Accordingly, he steadily bought D-marks and sold pounds to the tune of, by the end of August, $1.5bn.

The next significant pressure point came on Friday 11 September when the lira fell through the bottom of its ERM band. The subsequent weekend Italian devaluation, followed by a small Bundesbank rate cut, generated another shower of profits for short-sellers and put sterling in traders' sights.

A British devaluation appeared less of a foregone conclusion. But currency expert Robert Johnson, in the process of joining Soros Fund Management, told Soros and Druckenmiller that he was 90% confident of a sterling devaluation within the next three months: 'So we felt like we might lose 1% or so if we were wrong,' he recalled, 'and we might make 20%. So, if you have a 20-to-1 shot…'[9] Then came Schlesinger's *Handelsblatt* interview on 15 September.

The Bundesbank president's 'unauthorised' comments made clear that he was not going to support the pound with another rate cut; indeed, he expected a sterling realignment. With no likelihood of a sustained British interest rate rise, a devaluation of the pound was virtually certain. As related by author Sebastian Mallaby, Druckenmiller recalled walking into Soros' office and telling him it was time to move. He still had the $1.5bn position against the pound opened in August, which he had been increasing since the conversation with Johnson. Now a trigger had happened, and he intended to build the position steadily. 'Soros listened and looked puzzled. "That doesn't make sense," he objected. "What do you mean?" Druckenmiller asked. "Well," Soros responded, "if the news story was accurate and there was almost no downside, why just build steadily? Why not jump straight to $15bn?" Soros advised: "Go for the jugular." Druckenmiller could see Soros was right.[10] By 4pm in London on Wednesday 16 September, Druckenmiller, Soros and their traders had short-sold around $10bn of sterling and Soros Fund Management was 'margined to the eyebrows'.[11] Soros explained later that the amount levied against sterling was less than the $15bn target he and his colleagues had set. 'Things moved faster than we expected and we didn't manage to build up the full position.'[12]

Sterling's devaluation after the ERM departure, allowing short-sellers to buy back pounds at much cheaper levels than those at which they had been sold, generated profits for Quantum and other Soros funds of around $1bn, around a quarter of the UK's estimated total cost to taxpayers. Other big winners were the hedge funds Caxton Corporation, run by Bruce Kovner, with $300m, and Jones Investments, run by Paul Tudor Jones, with $250m. Around $800m was believed to have been made by the currency desks of seven US banks. Then came a host of smaller hedge funds, mutual funds, corporate treasurers and others.[13]

In fact, the Soros funds' overall profits were considerably larger than $1bn, since Druckenmiller also took other positions related to the sterling bet. He bought gilts and British equities anticipating that lower interest rates and weaker sterling would push up prices, as indeed happened. Subsequently, he and Johnson conducted large-scale shorting of the Swedish krona, which duly devalued in November 1992, generating a further profit of around $1bn. Considering all these operations, Quantum made a 69% return in 1992. After Black Wednesday, the Soros funds did well, too, by betting on the view that the Bundesbank did not want a French devaluation and would support the franc. Accordingly, Druckenmiller bought French bonds, which soared in 1993, contributing to Quantum's 63% return that year. 'I felt safe betting with the Bundesbank,' said Soros. 'The Bundesbank clearly wanted the lira and the pound devalued, but was prepared to defend the French franc. In the end, the score was Bundesbank three-nil; speculators two-one. I did even better than some others by sticking to the Bundesbank's side.'[14]

Soros and Druckenmiller kept quiet about their profits. But the secret was revealed in October 1992 when Gianni Agnelli, the Italian industrialist, revealed to journalists that his investment in Quantum would make him more that year than Fiat.[15] 'I Made a Billion as the Pound Crashed' boomed the front page of the *Daily Mail* on 24 October, next to a picture of a smiling Soros, drink in hand. 'We did short a lot of sterling and we did make a lot of money, because our funds are so large,' Soros told *The Times*. 'We must have been the biggest single factor in the days before the ERM fell apart. Our total position by Black Wednesday was almost $10bn… So a billion is about right.'[16] He was, marvelled the US magazine *Forbes*, the first person to make more than $1bn in the span of a single month: 'In former times, powerful central banks could usually frustrate speculators. They did so by simply buying massive amounts of the weaker currency and flooding the market with the stronger currency. But times are changing. While the central bank can mobilise tens of billions of dollars, trading in foreign currency markets now runs to a trillion dollars a day.'[17]

With the march of the hedge funds against the pound, Soros started a trend that central bankers could neglect only at their peril. One of those principally affected was Bank of England Governor Robin Leigh-Pemberton, a believer in the ERM, whose last year in office was marred by the monetary debacle. Asked in a valedictory interview by Alex Brummer of *The Guardian* whether he was resigned to be known as the governor who lost the reserves, Leigh-Pemberton replied he would be seen as the governor in office when George Soros won.[18]

CHAPTER THREE

Serial crises

At one level, Britain's 1992 ERM crisis was one of a long series of sterling depreciations. They began in 1919 when the pound, which had nominally remained on the gold standard during the first world war, was floated because of the impossibility of maintaining the wartime peg with the coming of peace. Since then there have been a further 10 substantial sterling depreciations: 1931, 1939, 1949, 1967, 1972, 1976, 1981, 1992, 2007 and 2016. Under the restored gold standard between 1925-31 and then under the Bretton Woods system between 1946-72, this meant devaluation against a pegged rate – a development that successive administrations resisted, generating a tone of political crisis, most notably in 1931 and 1967. Since 1972 the depreciations have been in the context of a floating pound – with the notable exception of 1992 when sterling broke its ERM peg, arguably reverting to type. The magnitude of sterling's decline in these 11 depreciations, from the onset of pressure to the low point in relation to the dollar, ranged from 54% to 12% and averaged 30%. In the ERM crisis, sterling's decline from its ERM peg to its low in February 1993 was 26%, close to that average.

In nearly all these cases, sterling's depredations were part of wider cross-border currency upheavals, whether European or global. The Black Wednesday upset was exceptional because of its size and scope. As Lamont said after he eventually resigned in 1993, 'The finance ministers of no fewer than nine countries were forced to eat their words and either devalue or float. Five floated; four devalued; one both devalued and floated.'[1] (He added, somewhat ruefully, that in no country did the finance minister resign. Indeed, in one country – Italy[2] – the governor of the central bank was actually promoted to prime minister. In 1997, another of Lamont's finance minister cohorts, Bertie Ahern from Ireland, became prime minister for 11 years.) In addition, the events of 1992 – and, most importantly, the substantial involvement of hedge funds – formed an important forerunner of another upheaval affecting a fixed exchange rate system, the 1997-98 Asian crisis, with widespread international ramifications that lingered for decades.

Currency crises are a long-standing feature of the international monetary system.[3] Even under the famously stable gold standard the leading 21 countries of Europe, the Americas and Japan experienced 22 currency crises between 1880-1913 (though not Britain).[4] And then came the financial crisis of 1914 around the outbreak of the first world war, which heralded a currency crisis in virtually every gold standard country and many others. Of the 36 gold standard countries, 28 abandoned convertibility.[5] During the two turbulent decades between the first and second world wars, the set of 21 countries experienced 44 currency crises, this time including Britain. The peak year, 1931, saw currency crises in no fewer than 14 of the 21 nations.

The two and a half decades of the Bretton Woods era from 1946 saw a similar incidence with 48 currency crises, usually devaluations to a lower peg, among the group, with a peak of 12 in 1971 when President Richard Nixon discontinued the dollar's convertibility into gold. In the post-Bretton Woods world from 1973, an enlarged set of 56 countries (accounting for most of global GDP) experienced 144 currency crises. The peak occurrence of 12 crises occurred twice: in 1986 in a variety of developing countries, and in 1992 in eight European countries and four emerging markets. While less extensive and acute than the currency crises of 1914, 1931 and 1971, the 1992 ERM crisis ranks as one of the world's most significant episodes of exchange rate turmoil.

A 2014 IMF study covering 143 countries, mostly emerging markets, identified 208 currency crises over the post-Bretton Woods period to 2007. They were particularly a feature of the 1990s, which Paul Krugman, the prominent US economist, has called 'the Age of Currency Crisis', with 1994-95 and 1997-98 the years of greatest incidence.[6]

The prevalence of currency crises attracted interest by economists. From the late 1970s they were 'a major subject of academic study'.[7] For the Bretton Woods era and subsequent decades, economists identified three generations of currency crises, with the 1992 ERM fiasco marking the transition from first-generation currency crisis models to second-generation models.[8] First-generation models attributed currency crises to inconsistencies between domestic macroeconomic policy and a pegged exchange rate commitment. 'In the early currency crisis models,' observed Krugman, 'the channel was assumed to be essentially a mechanical linkage; speculation led to a depletion of foreign exchange reserves, which would then force the central bank to give up its defence of the original parity.'[9]

In a similar way, such misadventures can coincide with persistent budget deficits that have to be financed either by depletion of assets, particularly foreign reserves, or by borrowing – neither of which can go on indefinitely. Exchange rate misalignments more often than not lead to a forced devaluation to a lower parity or the abandonment of the fixed rate and the floating of the currency. The model fits Britain's 1967 devaluation, the floating of the pound in 1972, and the 1976 IMF crisis, as well as crises in other countries.

Second-generation currency crisis models seek to explain how a government that is not pursuing an inconsistent macroeconomic policy may still suffer a crisis. They emphasise not the mechanical exhaustion of foreign exchange reserves but the dilemmas of macroeconomic management. Krugman wrote:

> Loosely, a second-generation model imagines a government that is physically able to defend a fixed exchange rate indefinitely, say by raising interest rates, but that may decide the cost of defence is greater than the cost in terms of credibility or political fallout from abandoning the defence and letting the currency float. In this case a currency crisis can develop because doubts about the government's willingness to defend the parity force it to raise interest rates, and the need to keep interest rates high in turn raises the cost of defending the parity to a level the government finds unacceptable. The second-generation model came into its own in the European crises of 1992-93.[10]

Market participants, notably hedge funds, grasp the political dilemma facing the administration and may question its commitment to the peg in the light of other policy goals. In these circumstances a speculative attack may occur, and succeed, even though policy is consistent with the exchange rate commitment. There is thus a framework for a speculative attack, but whether it will happen and the timing thereof are indeterminate. But if one does occur, it may blow up quickly and unexpectedly, as with Schlesinger's inadvertent comments about a realignment of European currencies.

Third-generation models emerged from the currency crises that struck Latin America's emerging markets (the 'Tequila crisis') in 1994-95 and Asia in 1997-98, which neither the first nor second-generation models seemed to fit. 'According to second-generation models, devaluing or floating a currency gives the government freedom to follow more expansionary policies,' commented Krugman, 'yet in both Latin America and Asia currency crises were followed by severe recessions.'[11]

The Asia crisis, which affected Thailand, Indonesia, Malaysia, South Korea and the Philippines, featured combinations of the breaking of exchange rates pegged to the dollar, sharp reversals of capital flows and the collapse of banks, resulting in a credit crunch. Hence third-generation currency crisis models featured analysis of the interplay between currency crises and banking crises – 'twin crises'.[12] Indeed, some economists were sceptical as to whether they were really currency crises. 'This was a different sort of crisis from the one that had often been seen in earlier periods,' observed Glenn Stevens, governor of the Reserve Bank of Australia, on the 10th anniversary of the Asia crisis:

> It was not a standard example of a currency crisis resulting from lax macroeconomic policies, in which large budget deficits, easy money, high inflation and so on lead to a loss of confidence in the policy regime and capital flight. In those cases, the standard remedy is mainly macroeconomic tightening to restore discipline and investor confidence. In Asia, by contrast, fiscal and monetary policies had always been reasonably conservative… At its heart, the Asian crisis was a banking crisis brought on by banks and their customers taking on too much foreign currency risk.[13]

A common element of the ERM crisis and the Asia crises was the role of hedge funds. The questionable sustainability of the Thai baht's pegged rate against the dollar came to the attention of Armino Fraga, one of Stanley Druckenmiller's lieutenants in late 1996 at Soros Fund Management. Fraga was alerted to it by a talk by Stanley Fischer, the second-in-command at the IMF.[14] In January 1997 Druckenmiller sold $2bn worth of the Thai currency and subsequently raised the short position to $3bn. This was a much smaller bet than the Quantum funds' potential position or the $10bn position they had taken against sterling, reflecting unease about taking an aggressive stance against an emerging market currency. Soros eased his conscience with the argument that the position was sending a signal to the Thai authorities of the need to devalue in the best interest of the country and its people. 'As it is,' Soros wrote later, 'the authorities resisted and when the break came it was catastrophic.'[15]

By spring 1997 it was not just the Soros funds that had a short position against the baht but also Thai investors and other macro hedge funds, notably Julian Robertson's Tiger Management, which built up a $2bn short position. As the 'battle of the baht' intensified, Tiger took the lead in active selling, echoing Druckenmiller's role in the 1992 sterling crisis, until the Bank of Thailand ran out of reserves and abandoned the peg on 2 July 1997. In subsequent months the currency devalued by 32%. Tiger profited by an estimated $300m and Quantum by around $750m.

The Soros funds also took a contrasting long position on the Indonesian rupiah. This proved disastrous and wiped out the gains from the Thai short. One account reported that, overall, the Soros funds were believed to have made losses on their position-taking in the Asia crisis.[16] Nevertheless, Malaysian Prime Minister Mahathir Mohamad viewed hedge funds as a grave threat to his own and other developing countries. He accused foreign speculators – 'who should be shot' – of 'teaming up to impoverish the poor countries'.[17] In particular he blamed Soros, denouncing him as a 'criminal' and 'moron' and called for the banning of 'unnecessary, unproductive and immoral' currency trading. Soros countered that Mahartir was 'a menace to his own country'. Later, though, both men – mellowed by age and experience – made up their differences.

The Tequila crisis and the Asia crisis led to large IMF facilities being rapidly provided to crisis-stricken countries. Thailand, for instance, received a $17bn facility and South Korea a record $55bn. This contrasted with the Fund's response to the ERM crisis. 'Where was the IMF when it was needed to sort out a currency crisis?' demanded a *Euromoney* editorial.[18] The article highlighted the plight of Sweden and Finland, which were shadowing the

ERM but had no access to its channels for borrowing foreign currency to defend their currencies. 'Thank goodness for the international capital markets which were able to meet that need,' the editorial declared. 'But doesn't the IMF have a role to play too? Or is its managing director, Michel Camdessus, determined to turn the institution into another aid agency, as his critics claim?' Such criticism may have been a factor spurring the Fund into proactive measures in the European sovereign debt crises in the 21st century.

The immediate impact on the IMF's thinking was an 'abrupt shift' away from belief in managed flexible exchange rates. Although the ERM survived thanks to the widening of the intervention bands in July 1993, confidence in that type of system was severely undermined. 'In its place, a new predominant paradigm arose: the "bipolar" view, also known as the "corner hypothesis"', observed James Broughton, the IMF historian. 'Floating would work; irrevocably fixed rates would work; but in the bigger view, any regime in between would be tested by markets and would ultimately collapse… Although the Fund as an institution did not take an official view in favour of any specific regime, the bipolar view influenced the general tone of the Fund's policy advice in the second half of the 1990s and for a few years afterwards. Gradually, acceptance of intermediate regimes then returned.'[19]

Resistance is the usual response by governments to pressure for devaluation, as in Britain in 1992 and Thailand in 1997. This is because devaluation is perceived as a humiliation and defeat, as well as concerns about its effect on import prices and purchasing power. Governments are right to be wary. A study by US economist Richard Cooper of Harvard University identified more than 200 devaluations in the Bretton Woods era between 1947-70. In countries that devalued the currency, almost 30% of incumbent administrations lost office in the following 12 months, compared to 14% in a control group. He concluded that a currency crisis 'roughly doubles the chance that a ruling group will be removed from power'.[20] A devaluation was particularly bad news for finance ministers, with no fewer than 60% losing their position in the year following a crisis.

Cooper's study was repeated by Jeffrey Frankel, another Harvard economist, for the years 1971-2003 with an international data-set covering 188 devaluations.[21] His findings were similar: the government's leader changed 29% of the time within 12 months of the crisis, compared to 20%

in a control group, meaning that in the post Bretton Woods era a currency crisis increased the likelihood of a prime minister or president leaving office by 45%. Chavalit Yongchaiyudh, Thailand's prime minister, stepped down in November 1997, five months after devaluation. John Major's discredited administration continued until the next British election in 1997, when it was defeated. Whether in Thailand or the UK, politicians in the firing line can agree on one essential point: currency upheavals are deleterious to ministerial health.

CHAPTER FOUR

Nation apart

Europe's post-war economic and monetary integration up to and beyond the 1992 ERM crisis developed in several distinct phases. In most of them, reflecting a combination of historical, political and economic factors, Britain was conspicuous by its absence. Britain's approach to Europe is defined by and grounded in differentiation. Its experience as a member of the European Community, the EU's forerunner, had mainly been that of an onlooker rather than a full participant.

Britain's European divide runs wide and deep. The UK has habitually stood aside from a turbulent continent. In the last 1,000 years Britain has suffered neither invasion nor overthrow, nor has it been a battleground for foreign powers. The ravages of the 30-years war and the Paris Commune, the rise and fall of the Iron Curtain, the march of dictators, the shifting of borders and the sacking of cities have all been phenomena played out beyond the fastness of the island nation. 'We are with Europe, but not of it,' Winston Churchill wrote in 1930, 'linked, but not compromised... interested and associated, but not absorbed.'[1]

Hugo Young, supreme chronicler of Britain's 20th century nexus of painful European relationships, described 'the mythology of the scepter'd isle, the demi-paradise... Tampering with this blessed plot was seen for decades as a kind of sacrilege which, even if the sophisticates among the political class could accept it, the people would never tolerate.'[2] In similar vein, Stephen Wall, a pro European career civil servant who witnessed the ERM upset as Major's foreign policy adviser, declared 'Henry VIII's Reformation was as much a reflection of continental encroachment as of Roman Catholicism. However venal Henry's motives, he tapped into a popular sense of England's island destiny that has remained with us ever since.' In his aptly named *A*

Stranger in Europe, Wall pointed to the perpetual difficulties Britain has faced in extolling the EU's benefits. Germany could point to industrial exports and democratic rehabilitation, France to 'binding' Germany to its side and privileging French agriculture. But all Britain seemed to have was perpetual gripes over the budget.[3] Ian Gilmour, a senior Conservative minister, wrote that, far from Britain aiming to occupy 'the heart of Europe' (as some politicians such as Major occasionally affirmed), Britain's supreme wish was to be 'at the heart of every quarrel'.[4]

Other countries, too, have had their difficulties. In a sense, Britain's experience after the second world war was the mirror image of Poland's. That nation's borders shifted west to incorporate large slices of the eastern part of Germany dismantled after 1945. Yet Poland as a whole was judged to have become part of 'eastern Europe' within the newly constituted empire of the Red Army[5] – a yoke from which the Poles were delivered only when the Soviet Union crumbled. Britain moved eastwards on the continent, its armies part of the occupation forces in Germany, remaining in the quartered capital of Berlin until the Germans finally reclaimed their sovereignty with reunification 45 years after Hitler's death. But Britain's focus remained on the US and the West, confirming the Churchillian dictum that, left to its own devices, it would choose the 'open sea' rather than the European landmass.[6]

Consequently, the UK's monetary dealings with the rest of the continent have habitually been part of a wider struggle over powers and responsibilities, in both competition and co-operation with the two other largest economies, Germany and France. Fluctuating alliances within this swirling ménage à trois have been a constant accompaniment to Britain's European journey. The UK has generally come to terms, somewhat grudgingly, with the necessity of negotiating European arrangements and accords. They have been engineered generally on the basis not of togetherness but rather of the UK's built-in European estrangement.

The sense and reality of division are rooted in the vicissitudes of the past. At the end of the second world war, continental Europe's economy was in ruins and regional trade had all but stopped. A key obstacle to recovery was the lack of functioning international payments and credit mechanisms. In the absence of convertible currencies, countries made bilateral trade agreements with each other in which either trade had to balance or one of the parties had to extend credit to the other. By the late 1940s there were some 200 such deals in operation.[7] The availability of dollar liquidity was eased by the Marshall Aid programme of 1948-52, which gave rise to the creation of the Organisation for European Economic Co-operation in 1948 to coordinate effective use of the US largesse. This was the first step in post-war European economic collaboration.

The payments bottleneck was eased with the creation in 1950 of the European Payments Union, which provided a mechanism for netting off inconvertible currency balances among 18 European countries so that only the overall net balance had to be settled. This facilitated the revival of European trade which eventually allowed a joint move to convertible currencies in Europe in 1958. Having successfully fulfilled its mission, the EPU was wound up in 1960. At the same time the OEEC was reinvented as the more broadly-based Organisation for Economic Co-operation and Development.

This regional progress took place within the international framework of the institutions formulated at the Bretton Woods conference of 1944: the International Monetary Fund, the World Bank, and the General Agreement on Tariffs and Trade that became operational from 1946. The key institution in the monetary sphere was the IMF, which had responsibility for monitoring and assisting the operation of the Bretton Woods system of fixed exchange rates. The dollar was the system's pivotal currency, though sterling remained the second international key currency into the 1960s, contributing to a British currency role and policy outlook very different to that of other European currencies.[8] After a bout of parity adjustment in the late 1940s – mostly the devaluation of European currencies against the dollar – currencies were largely stable within the Bretton Woods framework from the early 1950s until the late 1960s, helping the rapid expansion of world trade.

From the late 1950s and throughout the 1960s Europe progressed through the elimination of internal trade barriers and adoption of a common system of agricultural subsidies among the subset of countries that (without the UK) launched the European Economic Community. The generally stable and growing European and world economy provided the essential framework for the Treaty of Rome, signed in 1957 by Belgium, France, Germany, Italy, the Netherlands and Luxembourg, to establish the EEC, which became the European Community from 1967 and then the EU after 1992. The EEC's practical programme was the creation of a customs union ('common market') and the Common Agricultural Policy, which became operational in 1964. But the founders' ambition went further, with explicit mention in the treaty of members' balance of payments and exchange rate policy as a 'common concern'[9] – even though under the Bretton Woods rules these matters were principally the purview of the IMF.

The British decision to stay outside the Community in the 1950s was founded on the belief that the country's history was more glorious, its constitution more stable, and its people less willing to be led astray than those elsewhere. A decade or so later, the British were drawn in towards Europe for fear of being left behind economically by a grouping that had been manifestly more successful in mastering post-war rebuilding.

The EEC's progress and the constant search for currency stability in Europe led to adoption, in 1970, of the goal of economic and monetary union by the end of the decade. After the 1971-73 breakdown of the Bretton Woods system and the 1973 oil shock, that objective proved unrealisable. The focus of the 1970s was on the establishment of a regional Bretton Woods arrangement – the European snake – to create a zone of exchange rate stability. Britain played no part in these moves up to 1972, when it fleetingly joined the snake. Even with accession to the Community in 1973, the UK largely pursued its own path. From 1979, in addition to a revamped snake arrangement, the EMU vision re-emerged through the establishment of the European Monetary System, set up as a result of co-operation between West German Chancellor Helmut Schmidt and French President Valéry Giscard d'Estaing. Britain was a member of the EMS in a formal sense but stayed outside the scheme's fundamental element, the ERM, until it joined in 1990 after an ill-fated attempt to bring sterling's exchange rate in line with the D-mark.

The process of European adhesion, contorted and accident-strewn as it turned out to be, if anything swelled the impression that Britain was a nation apart. The UK's 23-month period of ERM membership marked a subset of the wider pattern. Joining the mechanism in October 1990 appeared part of a wider move to overcome European divisions after the fall of the Berlin Wall. Yet, in reality, the action struck a chord of dissonance rather than a note of unity – one more sign of the unyieldingly disparate nature of Britain's politics and economics.

CHAPTER FIVE

'This poor man'

Britain's attempt from the late 1950s onwards to join the passage of European integration came only after it suffered a defeat on the economic and political battlefield that was, in its own way, as devastating as anything that had befallen the nation in wartime. Prompted by dawning recognition of Britain's own frailty after the 1956 Suez crisis, Prime Minister Harold Macmillan launched Britain's campaign to join the common market. But he was repulsed by Charles de Gaulle, a wartime ally now at the helm of a resurgent France and supremely wary of Anglo-Saxon influence. The French president foresaw, with greater confidence in the UK's abilities than turned out to be justified, that Britain wished to refashion Europe in its image, just as the general was to shape the Fifth Republic in his own. De Gaulle believed the British were America's icebreakers. He seized on sterling's shortcomings as an excuse to oppose, and eventually block, the common market application. The UK was too financially weak to join the six founding members of the EEC. Shortly before vetoing British membership, he described Macmillan to his ministers as 'this poor man, to whom I have nothing to give.'[1]

De Gaulle's hold ebbed during the 1960s as Germany's economic success grew and Britain, from the sidelines, persisted in seeking – and eventually gained – the attention of the other major European powers. The revaluation of the D-mark in 1961, the first indication of the currency's march to hard-money status, confirmed the widening gap in Germany's economic performance with that of France and the UK. Partly in reaction to this, France started to assemble the building blocks for a European currency. Robert Marjolin, the French member of the European Commission, the EEC's executive body, proclaimed that currency disturbances undermined the common market, telling EEC central bank governors in October 1964 to prepare for monetary unification. Arguing exchange rate flexibility was necessary to counter inflation, the Bundesbank treated the Commission's suggestions with disdain. So did the Nederlandsche Bank, the Dutch central bank, which by joining in the 1961 D-mark revaluation was confirmed as the Bundesbank's closest European ally. This was the beginning of a schism between different monetary factions, setting the tone for decades of infighting.

Bundesbank President Karl Blessing, in a precursor of German arguments that would resonate into the 21st century, maintained that monetary union required 'a common trade policy, a common finance and budget policy, a common economic policy, a common social and wage policy – a common policy all round.'[2] In October 1962, Blessing sent a secret letter to Lord Cromer, governor of the Bank of England, enclosing a copy of the French commissioner's proposals on monetary union, recording, 'The governors [have come] to the conclusion that Marjolin's ideas go too far and move too fast and that nothing should be laid down that would prejudice the British position.'[3]

The three-cornered jousting between Britain, Germany and France played a part in the unravelling of trans-Atlantic financial relationships as the fixed-rate Bretton Woods edifice headed towards breakdown. France started to transfer into gold its large dollar reserves accumulated during a run of payments surpluses. De Gaulle was attempting a quadruple coup – establishing French monetary leadership of Europe, eclipsing the British, shoring up the international status of gold, and striking against US hegemony. Between 1958-66 France acquired an average 400 tonnes of gold annually, regaining its traditional ascendancy over Germany's official gold holdings. Yet, by undermining a cornerstone of Bretton Woods, the French president helped accelerate the progressive collapse of the world monetary system that ultimately contributed to his own downfall.

At the end of a long and fruitless effort to stave off sterling's decline, in November 1967 Harold Wilson's Labour government was forced to carry out a 14.7% devaluation. The pound eventually stabilised, and the foreign exchange markets spotted a new target: the franc, which had become substantially overvalued against the D-mark as the result of high French production costs. Social unrest that erupted with the student revolts of May

1968 triggered an intense bout of franc selling. The Bundesbank favoured an upward shift in the German currency, initially blocked by the Bonn 'grand coalition' government. In April 1969, de Gaulle resigned after the unfavourable outcome of a referendum on regional policies. His successor Georges Pompidou launched a much more pragmatic policy towards the US and France's long-suffering European allies.

Pompidou, like Emmanuel Macron, elected in May 2017 as the eighth president of the Fifth Republic, worked previously for the Rothschild merchant bank. Pompidou appointed as prime minister Jacques Chaban-Delmas, a progressive Gaullist Resistance hero sporting ideas for a unifying 'new society' bridging traditional divisions between left and right, managers and workers, young and old. Chaban-Delmas' magisterial – but ultimately fruitless – inaugural speech to the National Assembly in June 1969 served as a prototype for many future French reformists: 'Our society must show solidarity with social groups and individuals affected by economic transformation. Our government will combine reconciliation and action.'[4] Pompidou died in 1974 from a cancer already diagnosed when he took power, his grand ambitions snuffed out by the 1973-74 oil shock triggered by the Yom Kippur Arab-Israeli war. All Pompidou's successors campaigned on platforms of national renaissance; none fulfilled initial hopes.

Pompidou's monetary baptism of fire was the prelude to many future upsets. As capital flowed into Germany in expectation of a D-mark revaluation, Valéry Giscard d'Estaing, Pompidou's finance minister, devalued the franc 11.1% in August 1969. This was the first of Giscard's three progressively more humiliating currency downgrades during the seven years to 1976, an essential part of France's migration towards monetary union. Increased expectations of a D-mark revaluation came to a head after the September 1969 West German general election, resulting in the Bundesbank getting its way with a 9.3% revaluation of the D-mark the following month.

The currency changes disrupted the common market and the Common Agricultural Policy, and highlighted Europe's need for a more permanent means for maintaining exchange rate stability. By then, ahead of schedule, the Community's internal tariffs and quotas had been virtually dismantled, forging a genuine common market in traded goods. Europe's political leaders wished to maintain the momentum towards economic integration, but emerging imbalances were inimical to this goal. The 1969 manoeuvring confirmed the Bundesbank as a prime monetary force, in charge of an economy that had re-emerged as Europe's powerhouse. France's concern about Germany's size and prowess was all-pervasive. In March 1969, a month before his 11-year presidency ended, a badly weakened de Gaulle told Kurt Georg Kiesinger, West German chancellor, 'France has a certain hesitancy and caution regarding Germany's economic strength, as it does not wish to be inundated by German industry... With its entrepreneurs, its population and its infrastructure, it is best equipped for production, trade and especially export... In France there is nothing to compare... In industry and trade, Germany is in the lead.'[5] Michel Debré, de Gaulle's foreign minister, wrote: 'In November 1968 the strength of the [D-mark] permitted Germany for the first time to speak with a very loud voice. This strength ensured it the economic supremacy that made it the master of Europe for a very long time.'[6]

Balance of power arguments were back in fashion. France's entrenched sense of inferiority towards Germany provided the conditions that eventually brought Georges Pompidou, de Gaulle's successor, to lead the British into the Community. Pompidou's pendant in Bonn was Willy Brandt, who in 1969 became the post-war German state's first social democratic leader – a man whose vision was to rebuild West Germany's relations with the Soviet Union and eastern Europe, rather than to shine in monetary or economic affairs. In London, Pompidou found a willing interlocutor with Edward Heath, who became prime minister in 1970, a pro-European veteran of Britain's earlier fruitless attempt to join the Community under Macmillan.

By 1970, the French regarded Britain as a counterweight to Germany's growing strength, and the Germans believed that a tie-up with the UK would show France that Bonn's attentions were not universally geared to the East. At a meeting of European leaders in The Hague in December 1969, Pompidou abandoned de Gaulle's anti-British blockade, launching the EEC's first expansion, designed to bring in Britain, Ireland, Denmark and Norway – the first of six membership extensions up to the 21st century.

At the same time, the EEC Six set about constructing a detailed blueprint for economic and monetary union, drawn up under the stewardship of Luxembourg Prime Minister Pierre Werner. The Werner report of October 1970 proposed a series of stages culminating in the 'total and irreversible...

elimination of fluctuation in exchange rates, the irrevocable fixing of parity rates and the complete liberation of movements of capital' – all by 1980.[7] This was ambitious, but was nonetheless endorsed by political leaders in early 1971. Germany's demands for tightly-coordinated European economic policy required much more supranational decision-making than the French were prepared to concede. France's desire for speedy moves towards currency fixing and reserve pooling collided with a dawning German belief that more currency flexibility was required. These differences between France and Germany were destined to be long-lasting. Clashes were inevitable, and the plan was later abandoned after the 1973 oil price shock exposed the EEC's entrenched policy divisions.

Brandt made plain that he understood Pompidou's reasons for widening the common market: 'Those who fear that the economic strength of the Federal Republic could upset the balance within the Community should favour enlargement for this very reason.'[8] As far as exchange rates were concerned, Brandt took his cue from Karl Schiller, his brilliant and acerbic finance minister. Expounding a policy Germany was destined to repeat for a quarter of a century, Schiller announced monetary union would happen only once European economies had converged. A Bank of England paper voiced arguments that would reverberate for decades: 'The plan for EMU… could imply the creation of a European federal state, with a single currency. All the basic instruments of national economic management (fiscal, monetary, incomes and regional policies) would ultimately be handed over to the central federal authorities.'[9]

In carrying out the Werner plan, Brandt ordered Schiller to apply orthodoxy with unwavering force: 'We should be careful to stamp our hallmark on future work to implement the Werner report in Europe. This offers the best guarantee that, throughout the Community, our monetary policy views prevail in the widest possible fashion.'[10] Germany's strictures represented a demanding requirement for economic discipline. Britain, and other countries, were found wanting. Troubles erupted in the US as well.

As Europe faced its first hurdles in implementing the Werner plan, President Richard Nixon pulled out a linchpin of the Bretton Woods system in August 1971 by ending the convertibility of the dollar into gold. The ensuing Smithsonian agreement of December 1971 resurrected the world fixed exchange rate system but with the fluctuation bands of other currencies against the dollar broadened from 1% either side of a central rate to 2.25%, translating into an overall allowed fluctuation of 4.5%. This was diametrically opposed to Europe's ambitions, resulting in the Community launching its own regional currency arrangement – the snake. This limited fluctuations among member currencies to 1.1% each side of parity within the Smithsonian 4.5% band against the dollar – the dual arrangement being dubbed 'the snake in the tunnel'. The snake also featured short-term financing facilities to provide credit to countries with weak currencies, encroaching on the established domain of the IMF.

As a result of the currency integration plans, Britain found itself caught in a complex economic and political nexus for which it was ill-prepared. The snake became operational in late April 1972. Edward Heath, the British prime minister from 1970-74, a lifelong advocate of a united Europe and a veteran of the failed attempt to join the EEC that de Gaulle had vetoed seven years earlier, was preparing to preside over Britain's entry in January 1973. As a mark of support for the Werner plan the UK, as well as Denmark and Ireland (also scheduled to join the Community in January 1973), joined the snake on 1 May 1972. This was the UK's first involvement with European monetary integration, but it turned out to be a detour, not a turning point. At the same time as committing itself to a pegged snake exchange rate, Britain was pursuing 'highly inconsistent' expansionary policy measures. These led to rising inflation and a deteriorating current account.[11] In fact, a month before the launch of the snake, Anthony Barber, Britain's chancellor of the exchequer, told parliament that 'the lesson of the international balance of payments upsets of the last few years is that it is neither necessary nor desirable to distort domestic economies to an unacceptable extent in order to maintain unrealistic exchange rates, whether they are too high or too low.'[12] The foreign exchange market drew the conclusion that, if the pound came under pressure, Barber would devalue. The test came quicker than expected. A sizeable run out of sterling took place on 15 June when a national dock strike seemed imminent. On Friday 23 June – after $2.5bn was spent defending sterling in one week – Britain announced it was leaving the exchange rate scheme. Leslie O'Brien, governor of the Bank of England, on holiday in Cannes, awoke on 24 June to hear that sterling had been floated. He was not informed, let alone consulted, about the decision – and found out only later about the huge drain on reserves.[13]

CHAPTER SIX

Europe of many dimensions

In British politics, 'Europe' as applied to economic policy is a multidimensional affair. There are always divisions between and within parties. Strong emotions seldom lie far beneath the surface.

Whichever major party – Conservative or Labour – was in power during post-war decades, policy-makers had to navigate departments of state that were often at odds. In decisions and negotiations over the exchange rate mechanism, the Foreign Office was always far more pro-European than the Treasury. This partly reflected another division, between economists and non-economists, and ministers and officials who believed political considerations should triumph over economic hurdles. Adding to the complexity, opinions sometimes change over time within departments. A Treasury that was traditionally suspicious of Europe and Brussels could be worn down by events, not to say failure of policies, and move towards a less hostile approach to UK entry to the ERM. That is essentially what happened in the 1980s.

During the 1970s, after sterling's brief, ill-fated adventure with the European currency snake in 1972, the Treasury was understandably cool towards the European idea of an exchange rate mechanism. The timing anyway seemed unpropitious. The world moved to floating rates in March 1973 with the disintegration of the Smithsonian system and the floating of the dollar. The European snake currencies floated jointly against other currencies.

Then came the quadrupling of the oil price in the second half of 1973, fuelling inflation and triggering recession. European countries reacted to the downturn with different policy responses that resulted in a widening of inflation rates. By 1975, reported French European Commission member

Robert Marjolin, one of the architects of the single currency preparations who conducted a review of progress with the Werner plan, 'There was no more talk of EMU.'[1]

As the international monetary system became more fragmented and unstable, the snake was buffeted by further upheavals. Italy quit in early 1973. France departed in January 1974, rejoined in July 1975, and left again in March 1976. Denmark withdrew in June 1972, but rejoined in October 1972, and Norway left in December 1978. Additionally, there were numerous devaluations and revaluations of members' parities.

The interchanges between France and Germany in 1973-74, amid a sharp rise in world oil prices, were symptomatic of the unsettled state of Europe. The Bundesbank was warning the UK not to return too quickly to the snake in view of the potential for currency instability.[2] The Germans were growing worried, too, about France. In a gloomy summary of Europe's prospects presented to Brandt, Heath and Bank of England Governor Gordon Richardson in October 1973, Karl Otto Pöhl, state secretary under West German Finance Minister Helmut Schmidt, revealed that the Bundesbank had spent DM5bn in September defending the franc.[3] France had lost 10% of its reserves within a week. 'This situation could easily recur. The alternative to heavy intervention and losses would be the destruction of the snake... The objectives of France and Germany in economic policy are not the same. The French are much more concerned with the expansion of their economy. Germany is much more concerned with the fight against inflation.'

Pöhl was a quick-thinking, fast-learning economics official who had started his career as a freelance sports reporter and then enjoyed a rapid ascent in Bonn after an early life stricken by economic depression and war. Aged a mere 43 in 1973, he went to the forefront of negotiations around the time of the March 1973 breakdown of the Bretton Woods system, underlining, for example, Germany's political interest in seeing the UK in a Community currency bloc. These episodes prefigured 20 years of eminence in which he became a dominant figure in international finance as president of the Bundesbank during the turbulent 1980s before quitting in 1991 after multiple disagreements with Chancellor Helmut Kohl over German unification. Pöhl's private warnings over the French were borne out when in January 1974 Valéry Giscard d'Estaing, as Pompidou's finance minister, declared that France was withdrawing from the snake, turning down a $3bn German credit offer to maintain the franc in the currency mechanism.[4] Shortly before the official announcement, Giscard visited Pompidou in his modest village home north of Paris to seek the president's views. Their conversation, on Giscard's own account, presents an unflattering picture of Franco-German relations:

Pompidou: 'And what will happen if we let the franc float?'

Giscard: 'Certainly not much. We will maintain our parity against all other currencies. But the gap with the D-mark will increase and, as a result of the price increases of German products on our market, that will strengthen inflationary tendencies.'

Pompidou: 'Can we stop this?'

Giscard: 'For a certain time, but that will become very expensive for us. And ultimately we will not be able to prevent the franc and the D-mark from drifting away from each other.'

Pompidou: 'Then we have no other choice. We will not waste our last reserves, simply to delay an event that is evidently unavoidable. We must leave the currency snake… At the last summit conference, I noticed that [the Germans] do not have much understanding for our situation. As soon as one comes to them with monetary questions, they react completely egoistically. They like to exploit their superiority.'[5]

Giscard blamed competition from the floating Italian and British currencies for the franc's departure. He turned to a traditional rallying cry, employed many times during tussles with the Germans: France's first priority was to to protect its reserves.

By 1978, with three of the four largest European economies – France, Italy and the UK – floating outside the system, the snake's future was questionable. Nevertheless, Germany and northern European countries persevered with the quest for currency stability, culminating in the launch of the European Monetary System in 1979. Their pursuit of pegged exchange rates despite all the setbacks was, marvelled US economist Barry Eichengreen, 'one of the most striking features of the period'.[6]

This persistence partly reflected strong German self-interest. Protracted upwards pressure on the D-mark was endangering German export competitiveness, jobs and prosperity. Pöhl, in the finance ministry, gained further in stature when his mentor Schmidt replaced Brandt as chancellor in 1974. Pöhl was sent to the Bundesbank in 1977 as deputy president before taking over (from Otmar Emminger) as president in January 1980.

Part of Pöhl's mission in Frankfurt was to overcome the Bundesbank's opposition to a new scheme – the EMS – for quelling currency fluctuations. Pöhl wrote to Schmidt in March 1978, 'If the D-mark's high valuation against the dollar continues, then this might not only endanger our economic recovery but also give rise to structural changes (transfer of production facilities abroad) that could lead to permanent massive unemployment. We must therefore have an urgent interest in sharing the pressure of revaluation on as many shoulders as possible.'[7]

In view of the German desire for 'burden sharing' over revaluations, it was natural that Britain should become embroiled with preparations for the EMS and the exchange rate mechanism. There was never much dispute over Britain's fundamental antipathy. Yet in 1978 expectations grew in the press that Anglo-German rapprochement over currencies was on the way. James Callaghan, Britain's prime minister between 1976-79, got on well with Schmidt, but this was far from being a sufficient condition for ERM entry. Callaghan, chancellor of the exchequer during the torment of the 1967 sterling devaluation, was understandably wary about fixed exchange rate arrangements that could turn sour. After many European summits and high-level discussions, attention focused on a Schmidt-Callaghan meeting at the West German chancellery where, according to much media speculation, the two would announce sterling would join the EMS. At a press conference, billed by many as the venue for a dramatic announcement, the two leaders announced anticlimactically, 'We have been discussing the situation in Namibia… '[8] Edmund Dell, a junior Treasury minister at the time who later became trade secretary, described how the Labour government could not afford another split similar to that over the referendum on British membership of the EEC in 1975. 'The politics of the question were clear enough. Joining the ERM would divide the party and the government. It could not afford to be divided once again on a European issue.'[9]

The institutional background, too, weighed against joining. In 1978-79 the Treasury, despite vivid memories of the 1976 sterling crisis, was concerned that putting the pound in the exchange rate system would deprive the British government of the flexibility of occasional devaluation. The Foreign Office strongly supported ERM membership. The Bank of England, according to Denis Healey, Callaghan's chancellor of the exchequer, was 'mildly in favour, since they thought it would exert a useful discipline on British governments.'[10] Healey's opinion was crucial. A conspicuously clever politician, he was also a highly effective bruiser, useful in times of strife, who had always wanted to be foreign secretary but was given the poisoned chalice of the chancellorship in a difficult decade. Healey described a decisive discussion in Hamburg with Manfred Lahnstein, state secretary in the Bonn finance ministry and later finance minister under Schmidt. Lahnstein explained Schmidt's motives: to limit the foreign exchange market's tendency to raise the value of the D-mark, 'thus', Healey wrote later, 'keeping Germany more competitive, and other countries less so.'[11] Healey recorded, 'I was fairly agnostic until I realised, from long discussions with Lahnstein and others, how it was likely to work in practice. Then I turned against it.' Lahnstein, years later, confirmed the accuracy of the remark – but said it was meant as a joke.[12]

Meeting in Bremen in June 1978, the six snake member countries committed themselves to establish the EMS to provide a 'zone of currency stability', bringing back the countries that had left the snake, especially France and Italy. The EMS revived the vision of progress to economic and monetary union, though this time no date was set. The new scheme set up financing facilities for deficit countries and a proposed European Monetary Fund (which was never implemented). Both of these appeared as potential regional arrangements that would compete with the International Monetary Fund, which was initially suspicious but soon came to terms with the innovation.[13] At its launch in March 1979, the EMS included all nine Community members, though the UK did not join the ERM and sterling continued to float.

The EMS was designed as a 'fixed but adjustable' system, where countries could devalue from time to time (just as they could under its more ambitious ancestor, the Bretton Woods system). There was a bittersweet element to Healey's and Callaghan's forebodings. As it turned out, the main problem facing British economic policy after the Conservatives won the election in May 1979 and Margaret Thatcher became prime minister was not sterling's weakness, but its strength – described by Otmar Emminger, Bundesbank president until 1980, as 'by far the most excessive overvaluation which any currency has experienced in recent monetary history'.[14] The ascent of Thatcher, who gained notoriety for ending free school milk as education minister under the 1970-74 Heath government, marked the beginning of a period of duress and success for the British economy. It was also a time when the prime minister would regularly sally out to continental Europe in pleasurable anticipation of finding adversaries. ERM membership earlier in Thatcher's premiership would have been incompatible with her free-market views but might well have restrained part of sterling's excessive rise. It is worth reflecting that, when Britain eventually joined the ERM more than a decade later at the very end of Thatcher's twilight period, and the pound weakened because of rising interest rates in post-reunification Germany, the UK showed itself unable to use the ERM's supposed flexibility – with traumatic consequences.

The EMS launch was quickly followed by international monetary instability caused by the second oil price shock, stemming from the 1979 Iranian revolution, and robust credit tightening by Paul Volcker, chairman of the Federal Reserve, with interest rate increases from October 1979. From September 1979 to March 1983 the EMS experienced seven realignments, but no withdrawals.[15] On average, parities were changed every eight months in the system's first four years.[16]

The change in Downing Street ran parallel to new leaders taking over in France and Germany. Thatcher's European relationships were crucially affected by the accession of François Mitterrand as French president in 1981 and Helmut Kohl as West German chancellor in 1982. For an eventful decade and a half, both men dominated European politics and became the essential forces catalysing the drive to monetary union.

Three days after Kohl became chancellor, Mitterrand told his interlocutor, 14 years his junior: 'You are young – this is just a phase in your life. But the two of us can serve our countries.'[17] For her part, Thatcher's stature grew as a result of the British victory over Argentina in the Falklands war and the international strength of sterling. The currency's role as a 'petrocurrency' as a result of Britain's North Sea oil production is sometimes exaggerated; other countries possessing oil did not experience similar episodes. A subsequent UK government study, commissioned at the suggestion of Alan

Walters, Thatcher's economic adviser, established that oil accounted for less than one-fifth of sterling's rise. The main factor was higher interest rates in pursuance of then fashionable 'monetarism' – efforts by Thatcher and Geoffrey Howe, her first chancellor, to control money supply as a cornerstone of economic policy. This was in line with the overriding anti-inflation mantra which formed part of the legacy handed down by Keith Joseph, her long-time mentor.

Thatcher – the archetypal 'bloody difficult woman' long before Theresa May, prime minister after the 2016 referendum – had a thirst for confrontational politics which she displayed in large measure over Europe. She was suspicious of demonstrations of Franco-German solidarity. The British prime minister had at one time represented the Conservative party's pro-European tradition. In 1978 she termed Callaghan's decision to keep the pound out of the ERM a 'sad day for Europe'. But during the 1980s Thatcher's European view turned almost wholly negative: 'A Franco-German bloc with its own agenda had re-emerged to set the direction of the Community.'[18]

Thatcher and Mitterrand had a relationship of mutual respect – in contrast to her slowly-developing frostiness with Helmut Kohl. Mitterrand, who famously described Thatcher as possessing 'the mouth of Marilyn Monroe and the eyes of Caligula', admired and feared her precision, in particular over the long-simmering dispute on Britain's budgetary rebate from the Community, which was finally settled in 1984. He told Henry Kissinger: 'She has a strong personality… She is not used to encountering resistance.'[19] Pierre Bérégovoy, French finance minister during the mid-1980s who later became prime minister, forged strong ties with Nigel Lawson, Thatcher's second chancellor, who took over from Howe in 1983. Bérégovoy pressed the UK to join the ERM so that, according to one of his key advisers, 'France would not be alone with the Germans.'[20]

Lawson, who got on well with Bérégovoy, aided by his command of French, was a former *Financial Times* journalist of brilliant mind and pugilistic nature, somewhat over-enthusiastic in his pursuit of monetarist remedies for economic problems. His friendship with Bérégovoy provided one of the early reasons for his long-term (but unrequited) love affair with the ERM. Another reason was that the second four years of the ERM, from March 1983 to January 1987, were distinctly calmer with just four realignments, on average one every 12 months, reflecting a generally more stable international economic environment.[21]

As the US persevered with interest rate increases, the D-mark suffered unusual weakness against a sharply higher dollar, which reached a peak in early 1985 of DM3.47, double its depressed 1979-80 level, forcing the Bundesbank into highly unpopular credit tightening. These European monetary fluctuations, combined with the dollar's strength, prompted a simmering clash of wills between Lawson and Thatcher that eventually contributed to their political downfall. In January 1985 when sterling was under pressure Bernard Ingham, the bluff Yorkshireman who was Thatcher's chief press officer, told a press briefing that the prime minister, as a believer in market forces, would accept the pound falling below the politically sensitive level of $1.[22] The Treasury, however, was of a different view, resulting in a story from *The Observer* that the Bank of England would intervene to ward off the humiliation of a $1 pound. In a partial reversal, Thatcher even sought the help of her friend President Ronald Reagan to support sterling. Attempting to stave off disruptive swings that could spark protectionism in the US, the G7 countries eventually took coordinated action to curb the dollar's rise, under the September 1985 Plaza accord.

Efforts towards better management of floating rates prompted Britain to re-examine joining the ERM. Thatcher had briefly considered the idea in 1980, in a gesture to Schmidt aimed at winning support for Britain's European Community budgetary plans. Lawson saw the ERM as a possible new monetary lodestar that would supersede his earlier efforts to control the money supply, which he realised by the mid-1980s had been an erratic and unreliable navigational guide.

In November 1985 during a meeting in Downing Street, Lawson, Robin Leigh-Pemberton, governor of the Bank of England, and Howe, who had become foreign secretary, all told Thatcher they wanted to join. Leigh-Pemberton, a country gentleman with a fine estate and a private model railway, displayed aristocratic charm and film-star good looks, making him an early Thatcher favourite. She chose him as governor over more obviously qualified candidates, although she later cooled towards him as a result of his progressive enthusiasm for EMU. Thatcher, not for the first time, disagreed with her ministers and advisers, summarising: 'Ayes seven, Noes one – the Noes have it… If you join the EMS, you will have to do so without me.'[23]

Lawson recorded, 'There was an awkward silence, and then the meeting broke up.'

Thatcher's opposition to the ERM did not prevent her from agreeing the Community treaty establishing the single market, the Single European Act – which laid down the ultimate goal of EMU – at a summit in Luxembourg in early December 1985. Both the UK and Germany agreed to inscribe the EMU objective into the single market treaty in a compromise to encourage other countries, predominantly France, to sign up to a comprehensive liberalisation that would include ending restrictions on capital movements.[24] At the behest of Chancellor Kohl, Hans Tietmeyer of the German finance ministry (who became Bundesbank president in the 1990s) told Thatcher during the Luxembourg talks that Britain's agreement to the treaty committed the UK neither to the goal of EMU nor to joining the ERM.[25]

Unknown to Thatcher, Britain maintained the momentum of European monetary manoeuvring. Lawson was as opposed as she was to EMU but believed Britain could treat membership of the ERM as a separate, technical issue to bring down UK inflation. Refusing to be blown off course, Lawson arranged for three top UK monetary officials – Peter Middleton and Geoffrey Littler from the Treasury and Anthony Loehnis of the Bank of England – to travel to Bonn in 1985 for secret talks with the West German government and the Bundesbank on possible British membership of the ERM.

Middleton was the perfect mandarin to lead Lawson's covert ERM drive. A pioneer of the 1970s-onwards brand of media-savvy Treasury stalwart, Middleton – incisive, enigmatic to some and with a wicked sense of humour – rose from press officer under Chancellor Anthony Barber in the early 1970s to permanent secretary between 1983-91. He managed the transition from the Conservatives in the 1970s to Labour in 1974-79 and then Thatcher, adapting to the undulating orthodoxy, whatever his private reservations.

Lawson recalled later, 'The Germans made it clear they would welcome sterling's membership of the ERM, which in their view would help to maintain the soundness of the system despite the weakness of its southern members (they were particularly concerned about Italy).'[26]

In the following year sterling fell to DM2.85 from DM3.6 as a result of a sharp decrease in oil prices. Heavy intervention was needed in September 1986 to slow sterling's decline – including Bundesbank action to support the pound through a swap arrangement under which it lent D-marks to the Bank of England.[27] Lawson claimed later that, had the UK joined the ERM in 1985, member governments would have taken orderly steps to lower sterling's value as part of the system's regular realignments. 'I was never in favour of EMU... It was a different kettle of fish compared with the ERM. I saw the ERM as a useful way for us to make use of the credibility of the Bundesbank to get inflation down.' Such an experience, Lawson believed, would have prepared the UK for the harsher times ahead. 'If we had joined, as I wanted to, in 1985-86, we would have had a period of five years or so when the Bundesbank's credibility was still intact before German unification, which we could have used to good advantage.'[28]

CHAPTER SEVEN

Shadow of the D-mark

European currency tranquillity was shattered in 1986 by two international disturbances: the arrival of a neo-Gaullist administration in Paris, and an accelerating decline of the dollar. In the March 1986 French parliamentary elections the unpredictable Jacques Chirac, a veteran of numerous economic policy disputes with the Germans, recaptured the post of prime minister he had held in the mid-1970s under Valéry Giscard d'Estaing. An uneasy period of 'cohabitation' started under President François Mitterrand – preparation for Chirac's own ill-starred 12-year presidency that started in 1995 after Mitterrand left the scene. These episodes had far-reaching consequences for Nigel Lawson and Britain's long running flirtation with the European exchange rate mechanism.

International funds poured into the D-mark. One of the Chirac government's first acts, in April 1986, was to break with the previous Socialist government's hard-currency policy by devaluing the franc. Sterling was caught up in the turbulence. When the oil price fell sharply in early 1986, Lawson and the Treasury used the opportunity to allow a gentle devaluation of the pound to boost export competitiveness, on the assumption that the fall in the oil price would counteract any impact on prices. However, Lawson found himself in the classic position of a British chancellor who should have been 'careful what he wished for'. The financial markets again lost confidence in sterling.

The question of ERM entry came up in spring 1986. Thatcher publicly ruled it out, saying entry 'would limit our ability to let the exchange rate take the strain in any future run on the pound',[1] echoing Labour's nervousness in 1978-79. During the annual meetings of the World Bank and International Monetary Fund in Washington in September 1986, Lawson approached

Karl Otto Pöhl, the Bundesbank president, for assistance. Pöhl was a suave Anglophile of charisma and complexity, possessed of self-esteem and an eye for showmanship, who had become Europe's best-known and most powerful central banker. He regarded many of his fellow central bankers as mere plodders prone to the weakness of over-exertion. 'He has the laziness of the intelligent man,' as one of them said.

To Lawson's embarrassment, Pöhl – who earlier that year had made a speech urging the UK to join the ERM – told him the Bundesbank would not hold sterling in its reserves, but could buy pounds to support the rate as agents for the Bank of England. At a second meeting in the Bundesbank's plush hotel suite Pöhl offered the UK a D-mark loan.[2] A humiliated Lawson became acutely conscious of the disadvantages of life outside the ERM.

In October, Lawson, with Treasury and Bank officials, made several more pleas to the prime minister for ERM entry – all dismissed outright. Lawson subsequently admitted that 1986 had been 'a terrible year for the pound', down 15% over the year. The next step in his attempts to change the prime minister's mind came in February 1987, when the big industrial countries decided that enough was enough in the exchange markets. After the Plaza agreement in September 1985, the dollar had fallen to a more sensible level, lowering concerns that its overvaluation would cause massive US deindustrialisation and a move towards protectionism.

After the adjustment, the world needed a period of stability. The result was a new accord among G5 finance ministers and central bank governors on concerted intervention to stop the dollar from falling further. Lawson, who got on well with James Baker, the US Treasury secretary, thought highly of the Louvre accord, named after the location of the French finance ministry in Paris where it was sealed.

The experience led him to embark on a policy that later became known as 'shadowing the D-mark'. This was Lawson at his most hubristic, when he could say about interest rates: 'When I think they ought to go up they go up, and when I think they should come down they come down.'[3] His aim was now to extend the same manner of control to the exchange rate.

For Lawson, aligning the pound with the German currency was intended to be a relatively brief trial run for eventual ERM entry after the next general election. Remarkably, the shadowing experiment went on for almost a year before the prime minister discovered what was happening. When in spring 1988 Thatcher finally woke up to what Lawson and the Bank of England had been doing, her ire was all the greater.

The story was initially broken – by William Keegan in *The Observer* – in March 1987, but was initially denied.[4] The essence appeared under the headline 'Secret sterling deal ahead of budget', with the following passage: 'It is understood that a secret target zone for the movement of the pound against the D-mark was agreed between the UK and West Germany around the time of the Group of Five meeting in Paris last month… It is thought that the Bank of England and the Bundesbank have an agreement to intervene to keep the pound broadly within a range of DM2.75 to DM3.05.' A fortnight later, *The Observer* wrote, 'The Government is now operating economic policy as if the pound were already in the exchange rate mechanism of the European Monetary System. Nigel Lawson would like to put sterling formally into the ERM shortly after a June election… '[5]

When Thatcher and Alan Walters, her economic adviser, eventually became aware of Lawson's currency manoeuvring, the results were acrimonious in the extreme. The prime minister did not like the ERM partly because it was European and partly because it tried to 'buck the market' – a policy she resolutely opposed[6] (notwithstanding her sanctioning of intervention in January 1985 to support the pound above $1). Walters regarded the ERM as 'half baked', since it was neither a fully-fledged single currency nor a fixed-rate system on Bretton Woods lines assisted by capital controls.

This was a sensitive time for Lawson. As a consequence of the worst British recession since the second world war, inflation had fallen to around 3.5% by the time of the 1983 election from a high of 21% in 1980. After that it had begun to edge up again, given added impetus by Lawson's expansionist tax-cutting budget of 1988. The economy was booming and Lawson was lauded by some as Thatcher's successor. Such speculation did not find favour with the Iron Lady. This could have been a springboard for Lawson's rise to the top, but the trajectory turned downwards. Thatcher's relationship with her chancellor never recovered from the 'shadowing' discovery. Walters' close ties to Thatcher added to the strains. After holding an official position in Downing Street in the early 1980s he moved to Washington, where he spent most of his time, but continued to be on call for the prime minister.

In 1988-89, he returned to London, a move Lawson saw as a provocation. Apart from hindering Lawson's persistent attempts to erode the prime minister's opposition to joining the ERM, Walters' proximity was a public blow to the chancellor's pride. Lawson was furious when a story in the *Financial Times* emphasised Walters' trenchant criticism of the ERM in an academic paper.[7] On at least one 'private' occasion in the City, Walters made his ERM scepticism known to a wider audience.

The infighting between Walters and Lawson coincided with a bout of European political and economic machinations over the single currency that added further to the complexity of Whitehall battles. A single European currency had been the object of dreams and deliberations over many years. Political pressure was rising from both France and Germany for more active steps towards currency stability. Hans-Dietrich Genscher, the long-standing German foreign minister, put forward plans in 1987-88 for a common European money to back the proposed single market. Edouard Balladur, Chirac's finance minister, presented a detailed proposal for reforming the EMS, building on a decade-long series of French efforts to propel Europe towards some form of harmonised money. Balladur, Lawson and Genscher took heart from the stabilising effects of the Louvre accord, and tried to extend them – with different motivations, and in very different ways.[8] The Bundesbank was a conspicuous critic. Pöhl, speaking to colleagues, termed as 'verbiage' Balladur's 'confused ideas' which 'made no sense'.[9]

On the issue of the single currency, the views of Pöhl and the British were aligned. Lawson did not support the long-term objective of economic and monetary union which he – like Thatcher – regarded as taking Europe in the direction of a single state that was inimical to British traditions of democracy and sovereignty. He kept this opposition separate from his 'long-term objective of full EMS membership',[10] even though the two issues were clearly linked. Yet, whether the British liked it or not, the monetary union project was gaining momentum. In 1988-89, under a plan proposed by Germany and France, the 12-nation European Community set up a central bankers' committee, including Robin Leigh-Pemberton, to lay down a potential route map towards EMU. The group was chaired by Jacques Delors, the mercurial European Commission president and former French finance minister. An accomplice rather than a confidant of Mitterrand, Delors regarded the veteran president's scheming with considerable suspicion, but saw monetary union as a prized means of adding to the effectiveness of the single market and also of at last bringing France up to the same monetary level as Germany.

Both Lawson and Pöhl, for different reasons, were highly critical of the committee, and especially of its leadership. Lawson later referred to the 'disaster of having Jacques Delors as the committee's chairman or even as one of its members'.[11] In the midst of the Hanover summit that convened the committee, Pöhl telephoned Kohl to complain about the decision.[12] At a Bundesbank council meeting on 30 June 1988 attended by Gerhard Stoltenberg, Kohl's finance minister, Pöhl told colleagues that the Commission's domination of the committee ensured that 'Latin' monetary views would prevail over German 'stability culture'.[13] On 4 July Pöhl called Leigh-Pemberton and the other central bankers to convey his unhappiness over the committee and Delors' role.[14] Kohl journeyed 10 days later to the Bundesbank council to tell the central bankers – in remarks echoing the plea for support of the EMS made by his predecessor Helmut Schmidt in a Bundesbank visit in November 1978 – of the overriding importance of the European Community.[15] Kohl underlined the importance of the Franco-German alliance, which 'went beyond the economic'.

The economic as well as the political background was promising for the new impetus for monetary union. The period from January 1987 to September 1992 was marked by the near-absence of realignments, with the sole exception of a devaluation of the lira in 1989.[16] Events in Britain meanwhile were proceeding in a direction that would not lead to stability but to an economic and political collision.

Lawson's tax-cutting March 1988 budget coincided with a credit boom that persisted for the rest of the year. When Thatcher found out about the D-mark policy shortly before the budget, she and Walters were particularly worried about the boost to Britain's reserves and the money supply of foreign exchange market intervention aimed at keeping the pound below DM3. Lawson could no longer hold the line, and the exchange rate burst through the unofficial ceiling of DM3 to DM3.1.[17]

The game was up. The prime minister and chancellor were arguing in public and hardly on speaking terms in private. Samuel Brittan, *Financial Times* economics commentator and Lawson's friend, went on television and radio to attack Thatcher for undermining him. Later Thatcher pinpointed

Lawson's D-mark policy as 'where we picked up inflation'.[18] She had learned from Walters and other mentors that inflation followed increases in the money supply. In fact higher inflation stemmed mainly from the more general 'Lawson boom' – credit expansion, tax cuts, faster earnings growth – and an atmosphere of near-euphoria surrounding an apparently successful chancellor. During the three months following the 1988 budget Lawson lowered interest rates several times to stem sterling's rise, without much impact on the currency, further stimulating an economy that was experiencing not only accelerating inflation but also a rapid deterioration in the balance of payments. This coincided with a move into budget surplus, thanks to booming tax receipts, which led some analysts to speculate the UK might, in the near future, be in a position to pay off the entire national debt. The shadowing policy, as an attempt to persuade Thatcher to agree to ERM membership, was a lamentable failure. Yet Lawson in 1988-89 started one last push to win her over. The backers included Geoffrey Howe, by then foreign secretary, and other members of what was still a predominantly pro-European Cabinet and parliamentary Conservative party.

There was no shortage of intrigue, on all sides. Thatcher was fascinated by the Bundesbank and by Pöhl, its president. An insight into the complexities came with Thatcher's journey to Frankfurt in February 1989 for a lunch date with Pöhl – the first and almost certainly last Bundesbank visit by a British prime minister. Characteristically Thatcher dominated the conversation with a tide of strictures on monetary union, turning up late for her subsequent meeting with Kohl – irritating the chancellor and adding to his slowly mounting antagonism to Pöhl.[19] During preparations for the lunch, Leigh-Pemberton, who had formed a close attachment with Pöhl during their monthly meetings at the Basel-based Bank for International Settlements and on the Delors committee, entreated Thatcher not to tell the Bundesbank chief that he had shared detailed papers from the Delors discussions with both the prime minister and Lawson. 'If Pöhl were to hear that, it would be bound to get around the committee very quickly and that would seriously undermine my position there. It has been agreed within the committee that committee papers and proceedings are to be treated as private. While I am sure that I am not the only central bank governor to have breached this convention, my personal position could be especially vulnerable to the knowledge that I have done so.' The governor added it would be 'immensely helpful' if Thatcher were to tell Pöhl that Leigh-Pemberton had 'done nothing more than discuss with you in principle the general questions.'[20]

Thatcher placed undue faith in the ability of Pöhl, as a known sceptic on monetary union, to block the Delors committee setting down a clear route to a single currency. As Thatcher was told in a Downing Street briefing note, Pöhl believed that EMU was not going to happen, but the Bundesbank president was not paying sufficient attention to the political momentum building up behind the process. 'Once these things are set down on paper in the European Community, they assume a life of their own. If the central bankers, who ought to know better, fail to point out... the very considerable difficulties and objections to EMU, they will find it much harder to restore the position once it falls into the hands of the politicians.' The paper suggested Thatcher should ask Pöhl whether he really envisaged 'the massive shifts of economic and political sovereignty involved in EMU taking place. Is he really prepared to put the stability of the D-mark at risk?'

Temperatures rose in June 1989 when press reports appeared that Thatcher was thinking of a 'night of the long knives' to replace both chancellor and foreign secretary. By this time interest rates had been increased in a series of steps to as high as 14% in an attempt to control inflation unleashed by the Lawson boom.

Lawson and Howe were far from alone in espousing ERM membership. It was supported by employers' bodies, the Trades Union Congress and influential newspapers, as well as a growing body of Whitehall and Bank of England officials. The Labour party had recovered from its anti-European mood of the early 1980s. John Smith, the shadow chancellor, and Gordon Brown, the party's Treasury spokesman (and later chancellor of the exchequer and prime minister), were both making positive noises about the ERM, doing their best to exploit differences between the prime minister and her two senior colleagues. Media speculation – some of it stoked up by Downing Street – about an impending Cabinet reshuffle forced Thatcher to proclaim in the House of Commons in June 1989 that she gave 'full, unequivocal and generous backing' to her chancellor.

The Conservatives did badly in the June 1989 European parliament elections, strengthening the Lawson-Howe position. By a joint threat of resignation – which she later termed 'an ambush'[21] – they persuaded

Thatcher to soften her anti-European tone for a summit in Madrid later that month. Lawson sought to mollify Thatcher by joining her in opposing rapid progress towards full economic and monetary union, as envisaged in the Delors report published in April 1988. The government reached an uneasy compromise under the so-called 'Madrid terms', saying entering the ERM would depend on the complete abolition of European Community exchange controls (due in July 1990) as well as UK success in bringing down sharply the 8.3% inflation rate.

The Madrid terms were essentially a delaying tactic, a prelude to both political and economic upheaval. The rumoured Cabinet shuffle took place on 24 July. Not Lawson but Howe was the victim, summarily dismissed from a role he manifestly enjoyed. For what would prove a remarkably short tenure, Thatcher replaced Howe at the Foreign Office with John Major, previously chief secretary to the Treasury under Lawson. The Treasury and Bank of England had embarked on a long process of raising rates to control the boom. But inflation had not fallen as hoped. Even officials in the Treasury and Bank dubious about European exchange rate schemes were starting to believe the ERM was the only way to beat inflation.

One of the fundamental causes of the credit boom had been the general philosophy of growth-boosting deregulation of which Thatcher and Lawson were so proud. But there was a fatal inconsistency in Conservative policies. Maintaining high interest rates to combat inflation was inimical to the government's desire to stoke economic expansion. But with floating exchange rates, declining interest rates would weaken sterling and add further to inflationary pressures through higher import prices. The ERM provided a potential escape route: a way to have the best of both worlds by keeping the exchange rate firm but allowing growth-friendly credit easing. By October 1989 interest rates were still at 14%, the trade deficit had already exceeded the Treasury's forecast for the entire year, and Lawson's 'economic miracle' had been unmasked as an illusion. The stage was set, in stormy circumstances, for the chancellor's departure – and a new path to the ERM.

Countdown

CHAPTER EIGHT

Reluctant convert

In his October 1989 resignation letter to Thatcher, Lawson wrote: 'The successful conduct of economic policy is possible only if there is, and is seen to be, full agreement between the prime minister and the chancellor of the exchequer. Recent events have confirmed that this essential requirement cannot be satisfied so long as Alan Walters remains your personal economic adviser.'[1]

There was only one circumstance in which Lawson would reconsider his decision to resign: if she were to sack Walters. In fact, Thatcher ended up with neither. Prompted by Kenneth Baker, the Conservative party chairman, Walters spoke to Thatcher in an evening phone call from Washington on 26 October immediately after hearing of the drama. He thought it best if he should 'step aside'. Walters was merely a part-timer, but that still gave Lawson ample chances for wreaking havoc. Thatcher would not sack him, so Walters sacked himself, but only under the party chair's guidance.

It was time for another helmsman at the Treasury. Amid frantic speculation on who would be the successor, Treasury officials fell prey to a classic misunderstanding. In an official world where people are often referred to by their initials, news spread that 'JM' was to be the new incumbent. At first officials thought this must refer to John MacGregor, a well-known and liked member of the parliamentary economic and financial committees, and a former Treasury minister.[2]

John Major, foreign secretary for just three months, seemed an unlikely first choice for the job. A decent and often underrated man, he never forgot his humble origins and outpaced more obviously qualified candidates as he ascended the Conservative leadership ladder. He was a great negotiator, not least over Maastricht and Northern Ireland, but his powers of conciliation were later sorely tested by Conservative Eurosceptics, whom he charmlessly labelled 'the bastards'. As the Lawson quarrel neared its climax in late 1989, Major shone as a competent chief secretary to the Treasury, the key minister responsible for controlling public expenditure. A year earlier, the prime minister had been reported (a story that was not denied) as seeing Major as her natural successor. Thatcher considered him 'one of us' – a true believer in Thatcherism. She seemed, however, to mistake courtesy for acquiescence. Major was a political chameleon highly adept at convincing others he was on their side, even though the truth was often somewhat different. It became apparent, especially when he took over the top job, that Major was much more of a centrist, 'one nation' Tory than Thatcher thought – and was strongly pro-European.

The Lawson boom was Major's inheritance, both as chancellor and prime minister. Two landmarks stand out in Major's year as chancellor. Having inherited interest rates at 15%, he kept them there for 11 months. He was also the man who finally wore down Thatcher and persuaded her to put the pound into the European mechanism. His year of chancellorship was overshadowed by the phenomenon drily described by veteran economist Lionel Robbins as lying at the heart of the economic cycle: 'The cause of depression is a previous boom, and the cause of boom is a monetary inflation.'[3] Lawson himself had written, 'People know in their bones not merely the immense economic and social harm that accelerating inflation is likely to inflict, but also how difficult and painful it is to bring it under control once it has it has taken off.'

During 18 years of Conservative rule in 1979-97 Britain underwent two recessions, but with a key difference. The damage during the early 1980s was felt mainly in the industrial midlands and north of the country, where the Conservatives did not have a natural electoral following. The downturn that befell Major in 1990-92, featuring high interest rates and the collapse of property prices, hit southern England hardest, where many Conversative constituencies were concentrated.

Ensconced at the Treasury, Major quickly set out his stall. In his first House of Commons appearance as chancellor, he capitalised on the inroads Lawson and Geoffrey Howe had made in Madrid. During the years before the pound joined the ERM, Thatcher's continual refrain was that Britain should join 'when the time is ripe' (or, sometimes, 'right'). The conditions now became more precise. Major promised emphatically that the pound would enter the ERM when the Madrid conditions had been fulfilled: 'We will join the ERM when the level of UK inflation is significantly lower, there is capital liberalisation in the Community, and real progress has been made towards completion of the single market... *But there should be no doubt: when these conditions are met, we shall join.*'[4]

Thatcher's opposition to the ERM was worn down by a combination of events. Her hopes of sabotaging progress towards monetary union had been thwarted when it became clear that Leigh-Pemberton, the Bank of England governor and British representative on the Delors committee, had 'gone native' and subscribed to progress towards a single currency. (By contrast, Thatcher scored a notable success with her championship of the single market, abetted by that indefatigable negotiator, Lord Cockfield.) The most important factor weakening her ability to battle against the ERM was that the Treasury had run out of options. Monetarism, monetary targets and shadowing the D-mark had all failed. The Lawson boom had set inflation on a path that was encouraging some officials to urge even higher interest rates than the 15% Major inherited.

Developments in Germany, too, were heaping pressure on the prime minister. Over the decades the British government has habitually performed better in weathering crises rather than anticipating them. The fall of the Berlin wall on 9 November 1989 provided a case study of poor performance in both categories. And it laid down a convoluted trail of causes and motivations for why 11 months later Britain eventually joined the ERM – and for why, in September 1992, it tumbled out. The seminal events across East Germany caught the UK establishment unawares – like much of the rest of the world (and most Germans themselves).

The initial reaction, epitomised by Thatcher's outpouring of angst over the prospective unbalancing of Europe, was an ill-disguised cacophony. The speedy unification of Germany provoked alarm and action as Europe's neighbours sought to adjust to the prospect of a larger, less constrained German nation. They rapidly came up with a primary method of damping the country's newfound continental power. The chosen route was to strengthen the pre-existing project for monetary union for Europe – catalysed by German unity to counteract its consequences.

All this posed a considerable dilemma for the Conservatives. The British government was split on the ultimate wisdom of EMU, with Thatcher viscerally opposed but leading ministers keeping an open mind. She was determined to resist. Her vehemence if anything increased after Britain took the fateful step of joining the ERM; in October 1990, three weeks after entry, and after other European governments had given the political green light to EMU (at a summit in Rome), Thatcher – less than a month before quitting as prime minister – succinctly summed up in the House of Commons whether Britain would join the single currency: 'No, No, No.' Yet one issue could not be avoided: the ERM was a crucial staging point towards the ultimate goal of a single money. Economic and political logic guided the British to an uneasy compromise – joining the currency mechanism, while ruling out any commitment to EMU.

The difficulties of that balancing act were increased by high UK inflation, significantly weakening Thatcher's hand just when she needed strong cards. For most of her premiership she had been fighting Europe in various ways, a continual struggle on which she appeared to thrive. Early on there were her demands for a Budget rebate – 'our money back' – from the dreaded 'Brussels'. The rebate issue was settled in 1984 at Fontainebleau. After that there were further skirmishes over the Delors report and the moves towards monetary union, with her fundamental opposition epitomised in a famous speech in Bruges in September 1988, when she said Britain had not 'rolled back the state in Britain' to be replaced by 'a new dominance from Brussels.' Thatcher had been warding off continual pressure to be more 'European' from Cabinet colleagues such as Howe, Douglas Hurd and Chris Patten, to say nothing of Lawson's tireless campaign over the ERM. Her change of heart over the exchange rate scheme was essentially a defeat. It coincided with a major domestic setback over her plan for a local authority poll tax, which led to demonstrations and riots in the streets.

Her persistence with the poll tax, in the face of serious opposition and well-meant advice, severely undermined her reputation. By 1990 she had lost her touch and was becoming increasingly unpopular, not least with her colleagues. Set against her was a new chancellor, Major, with strong views on bringing down inflation and determination to find a means to do so. Furthermore, he was determined to heal divisions with Germany – and making a success of ERM membership could be a useful step forward. On the inflation front, the annual increase in retail prices rose to 9.4% in April

1990 and 10.9% in September from 7.7% in January. Erosion of people's savings made inflation not just an economic problem but also a social scourge of the sort Major had witnessed as a child. He later commented that Lawson was 'not always sensitive to the frailties or needs of others. He did not know what it was like to run out of money on a Thursday evening, whereas I did.'[5] Furthermore, he was more concerned than Lawson about the effects on manufacturing of high interest rates – which Edward Heath, the former prime minister and long-time Thatcher antagonist, had described as Lawson's 'one club' weapon against inflation.[6]

Major had two advantages in his campaign to bend Thatcher's will. First, his position was intrinsically protected. As Oscar Wilde might have commented, for Thatcher to lose one chancellor over the ERM qualified as unfortunate, to lose two would look like carelessness. Second, in contrast to his predecessor, he was not confrontational. Major operated by building consensus and compromises. It was a painstaking process he once described, in the context of the Maastricht negotiations, as 'hard pounding'.[7] Douglas Hurd, who succeeded Major at the foreign office on 26 October 1989, had a similar approach. With notably more success than their predecessors, the two worked together to change Thatcher's mind. Hurd was a foreign policy buff with no pretence of economic expertise; he was too gracious to point out that few 'experts' got the issue right themselves. Hurd espoused the ERM issue for political reasons, not least because he wished to repair relations with Germany after Thatcher's well-publicised opposition to German unification.

The emollient approach of chancellor and foreign secretary began to pay dividends in May, when Thatcher exposed a flank. Reflecting some Treasury 'fine-tuning' with what it called 'the underlying inflation rate', she maintained in a public speech the Madrid condition on the inflation rate was becoming achievable. 'If you compare like with like, we are not so far above Europe's average for inflation.'[8]

Amid all the going back and forth, as far as the Treasury was concerned the definitive decision to become a member of the ERM was made in June 1990, although precise timing was still to be determined. An inspired report in the *Financial Times* referred to September or October, stressing that Major wished to enter at a relatively high exchange rate to demonstrate his counter-inflation credentials. On 10 July Major made the most definitive public statement. He said Britain *would* be joining the ERM, adding, 'That is not just my idiosyncratic view, that is the view of the British government. It is our agreed policy.'[9]

Officials most closely involved say the tipping point for the prime minister was when inflation reached 9.8% in June and July. One senior official recalled that every time he saw Thatcher from then on, she excitedly asked him when they were going to take the plunge. Some 15 years later Major told an audience at the London School of Economics that, in the end, Thatcher had been 'extremely keen' to join the ERM because of the seriousness of the economic situation and the recrudescence of inflation.[10]

The pressure for ERM entry had become almost insurmountable by the summer. From July onwards, the die was cast. A key Madrid requirement fell into place when the existing ERM members duly abolished remaining capital controls. One economic journalist recalls asking a senior official whether it would be safe to go on holiday in August. The answer was 'Yes, in August!' – a clear indication that a membership announcement could come shortly afterwards. Shortly before departing London to become Britain's executive director at the IMF in Washington, David Peretz, under secretary on the overseas side of the Treasury, sent a note to the Bank of England on 5 July stating: 'As more or less my last act in this job, I am sending you the latest version of the timetable we have prepared for the final days before entry.' The forward planning was meticulous. On the chosen Wednesday the chancellor would confirm with the prime minister and governor the timing, central rate and fluctuation bands for sterling against the other currencies, 'subject to market developments', and the Europeans and IMF would be informed. The announcement would be made on the Friday and markets would open on the Monday with sterling in the ERM. On 16 July Leigh-Pemberton told Major that he felt 'any suspicion of backsliding on the ERM could have a dangerous effect on sterling'. Major told the governor he had made a point of emphasising this to Thatcher.[11]

Thatcher was a reluctant convert. A letter from Charles Powell, the prime minister's foreign policy adviser, to Stephen Wall, who would go on to become Britain's permanent representative to the European Union, alludes to the halting and conditional nature of her transformation. In July 1990 Thatcher told a visiting Hans-Dietrich Genscher, Germany's foreign minister, that the UK 'wanted to avoid a row in the Community'. Powell wrote in a letter to Wall: 'We had therefore agreed to go further than she herself considered strictly necessary or wise, by proposing a common currency and a European Monetary Fund.'[12] But Thatcher never departed from the view that Britain's path was strewn with risks. Her mistrust of the single currency idea grew in line with the frequency of ministers telling her Britain should join the ERM. Thatcher told Genscher: 'A single currency simply did not make sense and would not be accepted by the British parliament.' Genscher said Germany was determined that a European Central Bank would be like the Bundesbank and entirely independent of governments. The best way to bring other European countries to adopt reasonable economic policies was to force them to submit to the discipline of a single currency and a strong central bank. Thatcher gave Genscher an intriguingly accurate foretaste of the pressures to which the Bundesbank would be subject, 25 years later, as one of the shareholders of the future European Central Bank. With some prescience, the prime minister declared she 'would have much more confidence in the discipline of the D-mark, based on the historic aversion of the German people to inflation, than in a central bank where Germany might find itself out-voted.'

CHAPTER NINE

In the dark

The exchange rate for ERM entry and the appropriate fluctuation bands were the subject of much internal Treasury and Bank of England discussion. The plethora of divergent views underlined the contradictions that lay behind the ERM membership plan. Britain wished to harness the stature of the Bundesbank to burnish its own monetary reputation and bring down interest rates. And it could profit from the perceived resilience of the ERM to put a floor under sterling, preventing any fall that would generate inflation.[1] Effectively, the British government sought to use for its own ends the de facto fixing of ERM exchange rates caused by a drive to EMU that many ministers fundamentally opposed and believed would not happen. This was a convoluted mix of policies, objectives and expectations. Not surprisingly, developments did not work out as planned.

The archives show that officials were examining every possible combination of relatively high and relatively low rates against the D-mark, as well as for movements against other currencies such as the lira. Some were happy with a high rate to show determination on the counter-inflation front, some were concerned about competitiveness, while others dismissed devaluation as a reliable method for countering balance of payments problems that could arise from the weak supply side of the economy.

Andrew Crockett of the Bank of England argued for a rate below DM3, with a leaning towards DM2.8 rather than DM2.9.[2] His colleague Anthony Coleby warned against setting the rate too far below DM3, which would lead to unwelcome pressure for lower interest rates. Pointing out that ERM entry was 'unavoidably a high-risk strategy', Coleby cautioned that the level 'should avoid incorporating the seeds of its own destruction. That proved to be the fate of the DM3 cap in 1987-88, because its preservation compelled the setting of interest rates at levels which were totally inadequate to prevent an explosive growth of domestic demand, which rapidly spilled over into the current account.' A crucial meeting of the chancellor, governor and officials on 31 August 1990, during the build-up to the 1990-91 Gulf war sparked by Iraq's annexation of Kuwait, dealt with concerns about the impact on markets of events in the Middle East and associated movements in the oil price.

The general view, amid intense expectations in political circles and financial markets that Britain was about to join, was that the government should abide by the intended plan, although a limited postponement should be considered – from mid-September to early October – because, as Terry Burns, permanent secretary to the Treasury from 1991-98, put it, 'Wars did lead to highly volatile markets.'

A tight monetary policy was seen as crucial and on no account should the Treasury decide to reduce interest rates before entry.[3] Warming to the theme that Britain should stick to its guns, Leigh-Pemberton told Major on 6 September 'a week or two's postponement was not a disaster' but, if markets believed entry had been put off because of persistent Gulf uncertainties 'we could suffer a loss of confidence in sterling' which could become 'very damaging'.[4]

As for the Madrid conditions, most notably that inflation should be a lot lower before joining, the Treasury and the Bank were at their most Jesuitical in provoking a rationale for a flexible interpretation of the policy commitment. 'Achieving' lower inflation was redefined as 'making progress' towards it. The annual UK inflation rate rose between 1989-90 to 9.5% from 7.8%, compared with a German figure in 1990 of 2.7%.

At the annual meetings of the World Bank and IMF in Washington at the end of September, shortly after the IMF had cast doubt on whether the UK was ready to join, a financial journalist asked Major whether the Madrid terms had been 'seasonally adjusted'. Major's smile almost gave the game away.[5]

Attention centred on Thatcher's insistence of an interest rate cut to 14% from 15% to coincide with the ERM announcement. The prime minister's demand for a quid pro quo represented a political trade-off. Thatcher would register a short-term gain in return for giving way on a long-term policy commitment on an issue – Europe – that had long been highly controversial. Around that time Thatcher told Kenneth Baker, the Conservative party chairman, who tried to dissuade her from joining, 'Kenneth, I have secured a 1% cut and when we join we will be able to adjust the value of sterling. I have been assured that we will have that flexibility.'[6]

Thatcher's view went diametrically against the advice of senior officials from the Treasury and the Bank of England. Eddie George, the hawkish Bank deputy governor, contributed greatly to stiffening the recommendations of Leigh-Pemberton, the generally ERM-supporting governor, who stepped up warnings against an over-hasty easing of interest rates.

George said later, 'I felt that there was not sufficient coherence among the different economic cultures. People in the Bank and in the Treasury would have known that I was less than enthusiastic. I was not at all confident that it would work. And it didn't.'[7] George eventually took over when Leigh-Pemberton retired in 1993. But his unbending attitude on the ERM may have been one of the reasons why Major initially failed to back George for the top job, preferring Dennis Weatherstone, the British-born group chairman and chief executive of J.P. Morgan – who, Major claimed, possessed 'greater presence' than George.

The built-in conflict between some of the UK's objectives came fully to the surface when Major and Leigh-Pemberton met on 3 October – accompanied, after a 15-minute initial tête-à-tête, by officials – to discuss Thatcher's request for the rate cut to accompany the planned entry announcement, now scheduled for 12 October. (The decision to bring the announcement forward by a week to 5 October was not made until the next day). Major said he had argued for a cut to be delayed until after entry and the upward pressure on sterling that was likely to follow. George warned that a simultaneous reduction in interest rates would undermine the strategy of entering the ERM to show 'commitment to firm monetary policies and not as a justification for bringing interest rates down'.

If he were faced with a straight choice between joining the ERM early with a simultaneous rate cut, or maintaining rates at their current levels and not joining, George said he would 'with great reluctance strongly advise not joining… Entry coupled with a reduction would carry a substantial risk of coming unstuck.'

Burns said cutting interest rates on domestic grounds just before entering the ERM was 'rather like the stag night before a wedding'.[8] Leigh-Pemberton said he did not like to 'take the dividend before the profit', a cautionary note that he repeated in a strongly worded personal letter to Thatcher the next day. Leigh-Pemberton's letter bore George's steely hallmark. The deputy governor had prepared a speaking note for the Bank chief which warned that, if the government gave a 'weak policy signal' by cutting interest rates at the same time as ERM entry, there was a 'small chance on this scenario of disaster – with a fall in the exchange rate putting upward pressure on interest rates'. Leigh-Pemberton's 4 October letter to the prime minister (copied to Major) repeated the admonition in diplomatic but decisive terms:

> There is a <u>strong</u> chance that such a move would produce downward pressure in the exchange market and this would increase the risk of pegging into the ERM at a rate which locked inflation into the economy. A prior or simultaneous lowering of interest rates would certainly complicate the entry negotiations, create confusion in the financial markets with consequent accusations that we had bungled an important policy move and there would be a chance, that we could not ignore, that we would have to reverse the interest rate cut. I see the fall in interest rates as a deserved and justified dividend from entering into the ERM and one that could well be distributed quite promptly after the event. I do think, however, that we should avoid distributing the dividend before we have been seen to have 'earned' it.[9]

The final decision to go ahead was taken on 4 October, at a meeting between Thatcher, Major, Burns, George, Peter Middleton and Nigel Wicks, the senior Treasury official for international affairs.[10] No mention of ERM membership was made at the immediately preceding Cabinet meeting at 10.30am, when the main items of discussion had been the arrest of two Irishmen suspected of terrorist activity at Stonehenge, the IRA bombing of the Royal School of Music College at Deal, and diplomatic manoeuvrings after the Gulf war.[11] Lamont confirmed later: 'During my time in Cabinet there were no discussions about the ERM.'[12]

Leigh-Pemberton did not take part in the afternoon meeting because he was already en route for a long-arranged trip to Tokyo where he was to give a number of speeches that were already part of a pre-arranged timetable. The Bank decided to go ahead with the visit on the grounds that postponing or cancelling the journey would have given rise to damaging speculation of an imminent ERM move. An important part of the meeting concerned the timing of the interest rate cut. George emphasised that the governor's letter of 4 October made the case for cutting rates later, since 'a simultaneous announcement would convey a weaker message… Risks were not symmetrical. If after the announcement the exchange rate rose, the case for a cut would be strengthened. However, there was a probability, albeit a low one, that the balance of the upward pressure from the entry announcement could be outweighed by the consequence of the lower interest rate.' Thatcher, by contrast, argued for acting simultaneously – and her view prevailed. 'She wanted to avoid the impression that the cut in interest rates was a bonus flowing from ERM entry – it was better to present it as fully justified by domestic conditions, with ERM entry providing an essential underpinning of counter-inflationary policy.'

Turning to the issue of the date of the declaration of entry, the meeting decided to abandon the original idea of inserting the announcement in Thatcher's planned speech to the Conservative party conference on 12 October, and bring it forward to the following day. 'The balance of advantage lay in acting as soon as possible. The exchange markets were stable, and the current exchange rate of DM2.93 was very close to what we would like the central rate to be.'

Communications ahead of the announcement – at 4pm in London on 5 October – were executed with a mix of precision and extreme prudence. Desire for secrecy severely limited room for consultation. One central issue was that, under ERM rules, the UK was committed to discuss with its European partners the modalities of membership, including most importantly the exchange rate. This clashed with the government view that joining was a sovereign decision. Wicks played a key role in contacting Mario Sarcinelli of the Banca d'Italia, chairman of the European Monetary Committee. There was a brief reference to the possibility of the committee meeting on Friday evening to discuss the move, but it eventually met on Saturday simply to ratify what was already a done deal.[13]

Senior ministers were kept in the dark about the move for fear of premature leaks. A Treasury note on the timetable for 5 October records an option for Major to inform 'selected Cabinet ministers' of the decision 'shortly before 4pm', adding a somewhat bizzare cautionary note – 'Or is this too risky?' – that underlined the level of ministerial mistrust. Geoffrey Howe, who as former chancellor of the exchequer and foreign secretary had been deeply involved in the ERM build-up, was completely sidelined. He was apprised of the news only on 5 October after he met the Queen at her Scottish residence of Balmoral and she asked for his opinion on the day's news. 'It did not take many moments to guess the point she had in mind. But long enough, I feel sure, for Her Majesty to have realised my state of ignorance. She must have thought it a little odd that the only member of her Cabinet who had been dealing with the subject since 1979 (apart from the prime minister) was apparently the last to hear of the government's decision.'[14]

The Cabinet did not meet for nearly a fortnight after the decision on entry. When it did convene, on 18 October, the official minutes record Major telling ministers that 'there had been a good deal of comment subsequently about the timing of these events, particularly the cut in interest rates' which he said had been 'entirely warranted by the monetary situation'.[15]

Major told the meeting, 'Against this background, it had been proper and necessary to reduce interest rates and the governor of the Bank of England had supported the move.' With masterful disingenuousness, Major told Cabinet the simultaneous base rate cut was necessary because 'a reduction in advance of entry would have given unfortunate signals to the market'. Major's account neglected entirely the discord with Leigh-Pemberton and George over timing, and was clearly designed to lead ministers towards believing the discussion had been about making an interest rate cut before, rather than after, the announcement.

It was not only the Cabinet that was kept in the dark – so too were Britain's Community partners, a tactic that came back to haunt the UK.

CHAPTER TEN

Taking the plunge

Britain's European partners showed much approbation, but also some disagreement, when a frenetic day of last-minute telephone conversations started on Friday 5 October to apprise them of the British decision. Major spoke to Mario Sarcinelli, chairman of the European Monetary Committee, at around 9am to tell him the pound would join at the central rate of DM2.95, slightly above the current market rates of DM2.93, and with the wider 6% fluctuation band (although the UK professed it would eventually adhere to the narrower 2.25% band). Major added entry would be announced along with a cut in interest rates. They discussed convening the Committee, which eventually met on Saturday morning at 10am. At 11am on 5 October Major telephoned Guido Carli, the Italian finance minister, who, although 'ill and evidently tired', said 'he was glad that the UK had taken the decision. The UK would be able to move to narrow bands more quickly than Italy had.'[1]

With Leigh-Pemberton on his way to Tokyo, Eddie George took over the task of informing other central banks of the imminent British move.[2] According to the Bank of England's account, at 9.45am George called Karl Otto Pohl, the Bundesbank president, to tell him of the 'proposed terms' including the DM2.95 central rate and the planned cut in interest rates. Pohl said he welcomed the decision but added his recommendation that 'the reduction on interest rates should be left for a couple of days, and that the proposed central rate of DM2.95 was a little too high.'

At 11.20am Major spoke to Pöhl. The Treasury account in the archives is somewhat different from Pöhl's own testimony, just a year after the event, according to which he remonstrated with Major when the chancellor told him that the pound would join at DM2.95. Pöhl, on his own recollection, said the entry rate was too high. Major said that the rate had been decided by Thatcher, whereupon Pöhl riposted: 'I don't care about your prime minister.' According to the Bundesbank's archives, which do not give details about the Pöhl-Major conversation, Hans Tietmeyer, the Bundesbank's international director, told his colleagues on the central bank council that the British had decided to join at a 'highly ambitious' rate.[3]

By contrast, the exchange rate issue does not appear in the UK Treasury account of the conversation between Pöhl annd Major. 'Pöhl began by congratulating the chancellor on his brave and courageous decision. The chancellor said he had decided that the moment had come to take the plunge. He was not keen to see a continuation of the frantic market activity of recent weeks.'

Telling the Bundesbank president of the plan to announce a simultaneous interest rate cut, Major said he 'would have hoped to avoid making these announcements together. But all the evidence, both published and yet to be published, suggested that we were much deeper into a disinflationary phase than had been fully appreciated.' Major emphasised he 'did not wish to promote the idea that entry into the ERM was a soft option or that the cut in interest rates flowed from that decision. It was also important not to mislead the markets and he would therefore be announcing both decisions together.'[4]

According to the Treasury note, Pöhl said 'he was not at all surprised by the decision to reduce interest rates. He might have chosen to delay the interest rate cut by a few days. But it was not an easy decision and UK interest rates had been high for a very long time now. Pöhl then offered to make a statement welcoming the announcement. He had avoided commenting publicly on entry into the ERM, despite misleading press stories, and he would continue to do so if the chancellor would prefer this. The chancellor said he thought a statement by Pöhl would be helpful.'

Philippe Lagayette, the combative deputy governor of the Banque de France, displayed somewhat more resistance when George telephoned him at 11.30am. 'Lagayette questioned immediately the intention to announce a proposed central rate. He argued that this would pre-empt the final decision of the monetary committee, which should be a collective decision. Any announcement of even a proposed central rate would be seen as a fait accompli.' George justified the announcement of the central rate by the linkage with the rate cut. Moreover, he 'hinted that, for political reasons, the UK proposal had to be undertaken as a package or not at all.'

Lagayette asked how the UK would react if the monetary committee opted for a different rate. George told him that 'we were not prepared to make our announcement in any other way'. Lagayette asked whether the Bank had spoken to Pöhl. George reported that the Bundesbank president, during the morning call, 'had been relaxed, although [Pöhl] would have preferred an interest rate reduction after entry to the ERM and thought the proposed central rate might be a little on the high side.'

Lagayette called back after about an hour with further reflections. 'The announcement of a proposed central rate posed a serious problem for the French. It was established EC procedure that the central rate should be subject to discussion and agreement.' He had talked to Banque de France Governor Jacques de Larosière, 'who agreed with Lagayette that the UK should not make any announcement of a proposed central rate before the monetary committee meeting'.

After consultations with Peter Middleton, at 1.30pm George spoke to Major, who by that time had spoken to the Bundesbank president. 'The chancellor confirmed that there was no question of changing our position to suit the French and that he would pass on this message if Bérégovoy contacted him.'

An hour later Pöhl told George that he 'shared the same concern as Lagayette but did not feel it was at all important, not least because he recognised fully the political aspects of the UK decision. He was quite relaxed about the proposed announcement and had no qualms with an announcement which proposed a central rate of around DM2.95.'

In a joint telephone consultation among European central banks at 3.45pm – just before the 4pm entry announcement – Pöhl put on display his underlying emollience towards the UK, with further important diplomatic efforts to smooth over problems regarding the entry procedure.

George opened the call by telling other central bankers that Leigh-Pemberton would have liked to speak to his fellow governors himself but had to go ahead with his trip to Asia 'to protect the security of the [ERM] operation'. In effective language that expertly synthesised the different negotiating positions of the Bank, Treasury and prime minister, George explained the entry level of DM2.95 and the simultaneous cut in interest rates.

> The terms of entry – with a relatively high central rate and the scope for upward movement in the exchange rate – are designed to ensure that we are in a position to continue to apply a firm counter-inflationary monetary policy. The interest rate reduction we believe is justified in its own right. There are clear signs now in the monetary data and in the wider economic statistics that domestic demand is softening. With ERM entry reinforcing counter-inflationary discipline we judge it safe to make this move. The lower interest rates should also help to moderate inflow into sterling that might otherwise occur if we announced ERM entry alone.

According to the Bank note of the conversation, 'All of the central bank governors (or their deputies) who spoke said how much they welcomed the UK application to join the ERM, although Lagayette predictably repeated his reservation that even a proposed central rate should be not be announced before the monetary committee.' Wim Duisenberg and Carlo Ciampi, the Dutch and Italian governors, supported Lagayette, 'although this reservation was not put forward with any great vigour and Pöhl smoothed the waters by intervening to say that there was no need for anyone else to repeat it.' The Bundesbank president ended the discussion by agreeing that the procedural points could be discussed at a later governors' meeting in Basel. 'He emphasised the desirability of the UK joining the ERM and the important contribution this would make to the completion of the EMS and towards EMU.'

With the Friday announcement completed – to a general tide of positive responses at home and abroad – Major endured an acrimonious exchange with Jacques Delors, the European Commission president, on Saturday 6 October. The disagreement is confirmed by the minutes of the Cabinet meeting on 18 October, which record Major as telling ministers ERM entry had been 'warmly welcomed in Europe, except by the president of the Commission, M. Jacques Delors, whose response had been rather grudging.'[5]

In his memoirs Delors says he and Major had a 'stormy telephone conversation' on Saturday, when the Commission president stated that the decision to enter the ERM with an overvalued exchange rate should have been taken by European finance ministers and not by the technical monetary committee experts.[6] Delors termed the decision 'regrettable and even reprehensible'. He added: 'I didn't set the other ministers against him because some of them judged, for political reasons, that membership of the European Monetary System was a good thing. But we had a very serious discussion, and I told him: "We will speak again on this, you are coming in at a rate that is too high."'

The archives show that questions of German monetary policy did not play any significant role in discussions among UK and European policy-makers preceding the 5 October announcement. Looking back at the episode in 2007, Hans Tietmeyer, at the time of Black Wednesday the Bundesbank's director for international affairs and later Bundesbank president, said Britain should have read the signs: 'When the British entered the ERM, from an economic point of view, I do not know how they could have expected that this would offer an opportunity for a continued substantial cut in UK interest rates. It was clear that German interest rates were on a rising trend because of policies on German reunification. If the UK really wanted to cut interest rates, then they should have entered the ERM at a lower exchange rate, or they should have stayed out for some more time.'[7]

Fate conspired to bring Britain into the ERM just five days after the reunification of Germany on 3 October. The British government became inextricably caught up in the turbulence of the fusing of Germany's disparate halves. The UK aimed to embark on a journey towards monetary rectitude, but in fact was climbing aboard a vehicle that was about to veer out of control. On 18 September 1992, two days after Black Wednesday, Andrew Turnbull, the Treasury's monetary specialist, conceded ruefully that those who believed Britain entered at too high a rate had a point. 'Our entry rate reflected the position in 1990 and the priorities of the time, i.e. to get inflation down. In retrospect, the rate may have been too high to be sustainable and too high once the depth and length of the recession emerged.'[8] As the Treasury's international expert Nigel Wicks wrote later, 'The reunification trauma meant that the mismatch between the requirements of German and UK policy would be especially pronounced.'[9]

The British believed they were joining the monetary mainstream. In reality, they were entering the maelstrom.

CHAPTER ELEVEN

Hot seat

Britain's ERM entry set off a wave of approbation from the City and industry, tempered by warnings from Leigh-Pemberton and others that ERM membership would make it more difficult to pass on higher wage costs through an expanding economy. Lawson wrote, with a trace of self-importance, 'I warmly congratulate my successor [Lamont] on his signal achievement. If my own resignation last year indirectly made it less difficult for him, then so much the better.'[1] For his part, Major denied that the exchange rate move and the accompanying cut in interest rates were an attempt to engineer a mini-boom ahead of the election that had to be held by summer 1992. Far from considering that the ERM decision might provoke a recession, Major instead focused his attention on serving up economic stimulus: 'It's unwise economically, it's unwise socially, and I actually think it's pretty batty politically as well,' he said.[2]

Spelling out the implications of ERM membership in the House of Commons on 15 October, Major ran into a withering broadside from John Smith, the shadow chancellor, who – while welcoming the decision to join – lambasted the government's failure to reduce inflation to a level more convergent with Germany. Britain's diminished competitiveness at the chosen ERM rate turned out to be a major element both adding to the length of the UK downturn and strengthening the Bundesbank's case at the denouement of the adventure that sterling was overvalued. Thatcher had made a 'humiliating U-turn' over the Madrid conditions, Smith said, since inflation – far from proceeding towards the European average as had been laid down as a condition for joining – had risen to 10.9% against 8.3% in June the previous year. He claimed that Thatcher, the 'inventor of the Madrid conditions', was now 'their arch-destroyer'. Smith affirmed that the prime minister's reluctance to take part in a parliamentary debate on joining the ERM was because 'she would find it impossible to justify the abandonment of a commitment that she made to the House [on the Madrid conditions]'.[3]

Smith – who died of a heart attack in 1994, thus paving the way for Tony Blair to become Labour leader and later prime minister – had risen to prominence in the late 1980s in particular for his effective assaults on Lawson's errors over the handling of the economy and the discord with Thatcher's adviser Alan Walters. By pinpointing Thatcher's equivocation over the ERM, Smith underlined the divisions at the heart of the Tory party that were to haunt it for decades to come. At a seminar in 2007 marking the 15th anniversary of Britain's ERM departure, Charles Powell, one of Thatcher's closest advisers, said of Thatcher's fundamental view of the ERM, 'She was opposed to joining it on the day that she joined it.'[4]

Giving in to her ministers over the ERM in no way eased political pressure on Thatcher. Rather, it intensified. Geoffrey Howe, her former chancellor and foreign secretary, had finally provoked the prime minister's ERM capitulation. But her strident anti-Europeanism, culminating in her 1988 Bruges speech, proved the last straw for Howe, provoking him into resignation from his largely honorific posts as deputy prime minister and leader of the House of Commons on 1 November 1990, within weeks of ERM entry on which Thatcher and Major had failed to consult with him. And, in a dramatic valedictory speech, he set off a chain reaction which led to the prime minister's own removal from office just three weeks later. 'The time has come for others to consider their own response to the tragic conflict of loyalties with which I have myself wrestled for perhaps too long,' Howe proclaimed, inviting a challenge to Thatcher for the leadership.[5]

Thatcher was persuaded by her closest colleagues to withdraw from a leadership contest provoked by a challenge from Michael Heseltine, the trade and industry secretary and one of her strongest rivals. In history, however, the most obvious person scheming for the succession does not necessarily achieve it. The crown fell on the head not of Heseltine but on that of Major, the chancellor who Thatcher advocated to her supporters and called 'one of us'. Major turned out, however, to have a far stronger pro-European streak than Thatcher had bargained for – terming the ERM as 'a modern-day gold standard with the D-mark as the anchor', making a determined effort to repair relations with Kohl, and heaping fulsome praise on the German economic system as mixing 'social security with market discipline'.[6]

Major enlisted as his campaign manager in the leadership contest Norman Lamont, who had been both financial secretary and chief secretary to the Treasury. From here, at what turned out to be a particularly trying time, he was propelled into the hot seat of the chancellorship. Lamont was widely regarded as getting the job as chancellor as a reward for campaigning success. But he maintained, 'While I was hoping I might be chancellor, that was not why I supported John Major or ran his campaign. We never talked about it.' For Major the choice was simple. Lamont had plenty of Treasury experience and was still there. Lamont cut a dashing figure, a politician of great sociability with a chortling laugh and a penchant for 'getting into scrapes', who conversationally could be in turn charming and abrupt. Lamont found himself beset during his career by occasional exotic episodes, somewhat luridly depicted (and sometimes invented) by the tabloid press.

Lamont's biggest setback was Black Wednesday. This was a fracas for which he, on the Eurosceptical side of the party and – although in the Cabinet at the time – not part of the entry decision-making, bears comparatively little blame. Lamont favoured flexible exchange rates, but admitted he had no idea that ERM membership would have such consequences. 'My own attitude was ambivalent. I was not involved in the decision to join... the day we joined I met a senior civil servant and said to him, "What have we done this for?" And he replied, "Oh, for political reasons."'[7] He fought a losing battle over an ERM policy in which he did not believe, but will also go down in history for sensibly listening, following the exit, to Treasury and Bank of England advice on more realistic economic policies.

Lamont became increasingly uneasy as the 1990-92 recession took its toll, all the more so since he was now responsible for it. The policy he inherited was essentially one of using the discipline of the ERM to bring inflation down. But when it later became clear the policy was proving politically, economically and socially disastrous, and normal prudence would have pointed to the need for a marked easing of the squeeze, he would ask his senior officials, 'Why are we conducting this policy?' Years later he said, 'I remember saying we should suspend our membership to a senior civil servant, and he said: "This was in your manifesto in 1979, decided by the previous prime minister, the present prime minister, [and] the man who was foreign secretary then and now [Douglas Hurd]. We've been in for a year and a half – what makes you think you've got the right to abandon it?"[8] Having accepted the poisoned chalice of the ERM, Lamont did not resign. As the recession mounted, a civil servant colleague summed up Lamont's position simply: the Treasury had lost Lawson, and 'we can't afford to lose another chancellor'.

Lamont lasted as chancellor from November 1990 to May 1993. The recession was aggravated by the constraints of ERM membership. Major, when chancellor, had coined the phrase, 'If the policy isn't hurting, it isn't working.' Lamont added his own embellishment. As unemployment soared for most of his chancellorship Lamont claimed that, in the fight against inflation, unemployment was a price 'well worth paying'.

From spring 1991 onwards Lamont promised economic recovery later in the year. He neutralised the impact of the poll tax that had contributed to Thatcher's downfall by raising VAT in the March 1991 budget – a move Philip Stephens, the *Financial Times* commentator, noted 'was not calculated to rekindle the consumer confidence the economy so badly needed'. In effect Lamont and the Treasury were trying to have the best of both worlds: promoting recovery, while rationalising a policy that was not conducive to recovery. They were to proclaim later that the government was squeezing inflation out of the system, in a way that might not have been possible without the prolonged constraints of the ERM.

As Lamont put it later, the ERM debacle was 'undoubtedly politically very damaging to the government. On the other hand, there is an economically strong argument that we did get the best of both worlds – a very rapid deceleration in inflation from 10.6% in November 1990 to below 2% four or five months after I left office. We did that with the ERM, and when the mechanism had fulfilled its task, it then disintegrated.'[9]

This somewhat optimistic view was shared by at least one of his senior Treasury advisers. Lamont's rationalisation was that a more gradualist approach would have run up against political hurdles. In effect, his argument was that the ERM policy about which he had such reservations, and for which he suffered personally, got inflation out of the system in a way British politicians, without the ERM straitjacket, could not have done.

But these were interpretations after the event. The process caused damage and fatigue for all concerned. The Labour opposition, under Neil Kinnock, the leader, and John Smith, shadow chancellor, took great advantage of the opportunity to attack Major and Lamont, conveniently underplaying the fact that they, too, had favoured ERM membership. With the recession deepening, Lamont was faced with a censure debate in the House of Commons in July 1991, but again promised an imminent recovery. By the time of the October 1991 Conservative party conference he came out with one of his most celebrated, and most derided, pronouncements: 'The green shoots of economic spring are appearing once again.' It was a dangerous metaphor. There are no green shoots in autumn. Indeed there were none in spring 1992 either.

The traditional view was that governments did not win general elections on the back of a recession. This folk wisdom had to be revised in April 1992 when the Conservatives managed to win one against the odds, helped by a combination of clever scare tactics – 'Labour's tax bombshell' – while introducing a 20% lower income tax band. The latter, Lamont was in no doubt, reminiscing years later, 'helped us to win the election'.

While Lamont himself was more in tune with Thatcher's views on Europe, Major had distanced himself from his former champion by declaring, on a visit to Bonn in March 1991, that he wished Britain to be 'at the very heart of Europe'. To Thatcher and the Conservative party's Eurosceptics, this was anathema.

The approach to Black Wednesday in the first half of 1992 was characterised by intermittent sterling pressure and endless dithering in Whitehall, Westminster and the Bank of England. During the spring and summer of 1992 the prime minister and chancellor dug themselves in further. The exchange markets were unsettled for much of this period, as first the Danish referendum and then the impending French referendum on the Maastricht treaty caused much speculation about the viability of the prevailing pattern of exchange rates.

On 5 May 1992 circumstances were calm enough for the government to reduce interest rates to 10% from 10.5%, but after that the pressure mounted on sterling. In July the chancellor called a meeting with the press and City gurus at the European Policy Forum, held at the Queen Elizabeth Conference Centre, located between parliament and the Treasury. Lamont listed the achievements: inflation had fallen to under 4% from 11%, the interest rate differential with Germany had declined to only 0.25 percentage points, and the trade performance had substantially improved. 'I cannot believe that we would have achieved all this outside the ERM.'[10]

Lamont listed multiple options proposed by the government's critics as potential exit routes from Britain's economic impasse. They included cutting interest rates within the ERM, realigning the mechanism based on a revaluation of the D-mark, devaluing sterling within the ERM, reducing interest rates sharply and leaving the ERM, as well as leaving the ERM and reintroducing monetary targets to determine interest rates. Lamont dismissed each idea in turn as defective or illusory, even though the latter option was the one which the government came closest to following just two months later. The ERM, Lamont proclaimed, 'is not an optional extra, an add-on to be jettisoned at the first hint of trouble. It is and will remain at the very centre of our macroeconomic strategy.'

A Treasury paper 12 months later, recognising that 'fears that leaving the ERM would destroy our counter-inflationary policy have not been realised', maintained that the purpose of the speech was to warn against the risks of a change in policy. Leaving the ERM had turned out better than the Treasury expected – 'but that does not make the warnings wrong... It is risky to cross a busy road with your eyes shut, this view is not falsified fact that people may occasionally try the experiment and survive.'[11]

CHAPTER TWELVE

'Against German interests'

Germany's reunification marked the climax of a geopolitical dash. Chancellor Helmut Kohl succeeded in balancing masterfully the frequently opposing interests of his electorate in eastern and western Germany, and those of the fractious second world war allies, the US, Soviet Union, Britain and France, that still held sway over a divided Germany. Kohl's feat represented the career highpoint of a man who before becoming chancellor in 1982 had been, as a UK government document described, 'always under-estimated as a politician', making 'tedious' speeches, lacking understanding of economics, yet at the same time 'a big, genial man' with 'straightforward propositions stated clearly, firmly and often.'[1] One of them was to override opposition – especially from the Bundesbank – and stride ahead with plans for economic and monetary union in Europe.

A key component in the politicking over German unification – and the monetary measures that would accompany it – was the attitude of Mikhail Gorbachev, the Soviet leader. On 6 December 1989 in Kiev, Gorbachev told Mitterrand Kohl was issuing a 'Diktat' on unification, and said he was behaving 'like a bull in a china shop'. Gorbachev told the French president: 'Help me to prevent German unification, otherwise I will be replaced by a soldier; otherwise, you will bear the responsibility for war.'[2] On 8 December at a Strasbourg European summit meeting, Kohl encountered widespread hostility towards prospective unification from other Community leaders. Four days later the chancellor told US Secretary of State James Baker that he was supporting EMU even though it was 'against German interests. For instance, the president of the Bundesbank [Pöhl] is against this development. But the step is politically important, for Germany needs friends.'[3] The fragility of the tightrope Kohl was treading – and his need of friends – was underlined in January 1990 by a conversation between Thatcher and Mitterrand in Paris, when both leaders again voiced doubt and uncertainty about German developments. Mitterrand complained:

> The problem of reunification has provoked a psychological shock with the Germans. This has revived certain characteristics that one had forgotten, a certain brutality and an elimination of all other problems apart from those corresponding to their own preoccupations. I say that the Germans have the right to self-determination, but I say also that I have the right to take into account the preoccupations of the rest of Europe.[4]

Margaret Thatcher believed monetary union would be an intrinsic part of a federal Europe, in which the Germans as the inevitable masters would be a destabilising force. Mitterrand, although no stranger to fears about German domination, had much more practical experience of the Germans; while Thatcher was a schoolgirl he had been held prisoner three times in Germany during the second world war.

On EMU, he took the opposite view to Thatcher. While he, too, was nervous about Germany's greater sway in Europe, Mitterrand believed monetary integration was the best means of keeping the Germans under control. In February 1990 Kohl advanced further on a collision course both with the Bundesbank and, as it turned out, with the rest of Europe. Without consultation with the central bank, and without considering the sizeable international implications for the D-mark as the anchor currency of the European Monetary System, he decided at short notice to introduce the West German currency into East Germany. The move was a strategic gamble designed to prevent wholesale migration of East Germans to the west of the country.

As Kohl told parliament, West Germany was carrying to the negotiating table 'our strongest economic asset – the D-mark'.[5] 'There is no time to go by the textbook,' said Lutz Stavenhagen, Kohl's pugnacious chancellery minister, affirming that the 'dramatic' danger of disintegration in East Germany made the step necessary before the end of the year.[6] In fact, it took place on 1 July. Kohl's announcement led to an ominous rise of the D-mark. UK Treasury economists, in an internal paper on 9 February that was sent to the prime minister's office three days later, forecast that German monetary union would increase German inflation and lead to higher Bundesbank interest rates.[7] There is little sign that the note was taken seriously.

According to a later internal Treasury post mortem, 'The Treasury seems to have played down the relevance of German reunification to the prospects for the UK's ERM membership.' A related Treasury document, equally self-critical, admitted that Britain under-estimated 'the scale and duration' of the necessary adjustment to 1980s excesses. This was 'part of the explanation why we didn't reflect more deeply on the possible implications of Germans' reunification.'[8]

Thatcher expressed anxieties about the effect of German monetary union. She told her ministers: 'Aren't we lucky not to be in [the Exchange Rate Mechanism]. What's the East German Mark going to do to the D-mark?' And she voiced irritation about the Germans' cavalier attitude towards international repercussions of German currency union, pointing out the Kohl government had made 'no study of its implications or the possible effect on others'.[9]

For the Treasury, the rewards from the ERM were still held to outstrip the risks. Yet the warning signals were becoming more frequent. Rather than ebbing, pressure for higher German interest rates increased in 1991. German inflation rose towards 5%-6%, contrasting with decelerating prices in the UK and the rest of Europe as economies slowed. The Bundesbank ended a 13-month ceasefire by raising its Lombard rate by 0.5 percentage points in November 1990, reigniting increases in its leading interest rates that had begun in summer 1988 and went on for four years. The scale of German challenges was underlined in May 1991 when Pöhl resigned from the Bundesbank after more than 11 years at the helm. This was the climax of a simmering dispute with Kohl over what Pöhl considered the former's reckless financing of German reunification.[10]

Drama erupted when Pöhl's long-standing deputy Helmut Schlesinger took over the top job. The new president was a career central banker with a trademark image for austerity. He believed monetary diplomacy required action, not words. He prevailed upon the council to slam on the brakes. As annual German inflation edged towards 5%, the Bundesbank announced a fearsome one percentage point increase in its discount rate and a smaller 0.25 percentage point rise in its Lombard rate in mid-August 1991, at the height of the European holiday season.[11] The step was necessary, Schlesinger confirmed later, to counter 'the wrong policies decided for the exchange rate of the East German Mark'.[12] At the same time, US interest rates and the dollar declined as the US economy slowed sharply. German interest rates, having been three percentage points below US levels in summer 1989, rose in the next three years to six percentage points above American rates. This was the sharpest trans-Atlantic monetary turnaround in the post-war era.[13]

As Britain entered an exceptionally severe economic downturn, this was not only an economic dilemma. According to David Marsh in the *Financial Times* on 12 March 1991:

> Membership of the ERM requires Britain to match German standards not only in managing interest rates and reducing inflation. In other areas, ranging from education, technology support and management-trade union co-operation to shareholders' long-term relations with companies, Germany's post-war performance has generally been far superior to Britain's. The UK is now under greater pressure than ever before to adopt these German-style precepts for the organisation of industrial society... The severe pain being experienced in East Germany could serve as a warning. Replacing the East German mark with the D-mark subjected most East German industries to the requirement either to bring their costs and productivity into line with West German ones, or go out of business. Now that the sterling-D-mark link has been forged, the pressures on Britain amount to a milder form of those borne by East Germany.[14]

The UK was caught in a three-pronged financial and political trap. First, as Thatcher and Major had planned, the UK was able to cut interest rates within the ERM. But, as Germany intensified its own monetary squeeze, the difference between British and German interest rates diminished rapidly, making sterling vulnerable to speculative attrition, and preventing any further UK rate cuts. Second, UK inflation fell rapidly, so that – despite the fall in nominal interest rates – real (inflation-adjusted) interest rates rose sharply.

Third, British exporters reliant on US sales were badly hit by a sharp rise in the pound to $2, which made American sales prohibitively expensive. For all these reasons, Britain's long awaited economic recovery stubbornly refused to take off.

Europe's monetary travails increased after the Maastricht summit in the Netherlands in December 1991. Closely following the findings of the Delors report and the work on the European Central Bank statute by European central bank governors, the treaty laid down a three-stage timetable for monetary union by 1997 or, at the latest, 1999, depending on the accomplishment of criteria for economic convergence – inflation, interest rates, and budgetary and debt positions. The most significant of the Maastricht 'convergence criteria' was the stipulation that countries' general government budget deficits should not exceed 3% of their GDP. The summit agreed EMU would automatically take place by the end of the decade for all Community countries which fulfilled the convergence criteria (apart from the UK and, later on, Denmark, which secured exemptions).

Knowing that the German electorate disliked EMU, France and Italy hatched the plan to ensure that not only Kohl but also his successors would be bound to the EMU goal. Although setting no explicit path towards political union, the treaty established firm constraints for economic policy among EMU members, all of which were to have deep and controversial implications. It prohibited direct financing of public entities' deficits by national central banks, stipulated that neither the Community nor any EMU member was liable for the commitments of any other member, and stated members should avoid excessive government deficits, under procedures to be policed by European finance ministers.[15]

The Maastricht treaty enshrined additional Community support, through the so-called Cohesion Fund, for weaker countries that would face economic constraints from the single currency. These measures fell a long way short of the thoroughgoing fiscal redistribution for weaker regions that is normally available within industrialised countries' national budgets. And in coming years member countries of EMU increasingly transgressed the rules to prevent the system from breaking down.

The Maastricht summit saw a new spirit of Bundesbank-Bonn co-operation. Finance Minister Theo Waigel phoned Schlesinger during the meeting to seek his advice on the independence of the future European Central Bank with regard to the crucial issue of the external exchange rate.[16] Helmut Kohl, for his part, displayed ebullient self-confidence. At Maastricht he agreed a wager with David Marsh that the UK would become a member of EMU by 1997, the earliest date set in the treaty. 'The government always does what the City wants… The City will ensure that Britain joins monetary union.' He duly lost the bet, and paid out the stake – six bottles of wine – in 1997.[17] The timetable to replace the D-mark goaded the Bundesbank into action. Alarmed by accelerating wage claims despite a slowing of the post-unification boom, only days after Maastricht the Bundesbank struck back. It raised its discount rate to 8% and its Lombard rate to 9.75%, the highest ever in West Germany.

France, which had briefly cut its money market interest rate below German levels, was forced to raise rates again.[18] Mitterrand stuck fast to the position of his advisers that France could not countenance any change in the franc-D-mark parity, on the grounds that French inflation was lower than in Germany.[19] Underlining trans-Atlantic divergence, the US cut its discount rate to 3.5%, reflecting pressure for domestic reflation from embattled President Bush and his Treasury Secretary Nicolas Brady.

The Bundesbank's interest rate action, meanwhile, sparked an unusual protest from the Netherlands, hitherto Germany's most robust monetary ally. Prime Minister Ruud Lubbers wrote to Kohl in January 1992 saying the Netherlands was 'alarmed' by Germany's leading interest rates and strengthening recessionary tendencies… This is seriously endangering acceptance of further economic and monetary integration.'[20] Lubbers words formed an apt prelude for the coming misadventures.

CHAPTER THIRTEEN

Grumbling volcano

Britain's ERM problems were many-sided and deep-rooted. They burst out into the open in the Kingdom of Denmark. A slender majority of the Danish electorate, habitually sceptical about giving up national sovereignty in favour of pan-European masterplans, rejected the Maastricht treaty in a closely fought referendum on 2 June 1992. The vote disturbed the international ratification process and propelled financial markets on a route towards upheaval by triggering, just a day later, a decision by French President François Mitterrand to call France's own referendum for the autumn. Robin Leigh-Pemberton said the Danish vote marked a 'tremor': 'We knew throughout the summer that we were sitting on a grumbling volcano.'[1] Norman Lamont related how he 'leapt into the air' when he heard the news, 'an incautious reaction of sheer delight. Could this, I wondered, be the end of the single currency?'[2] It was not. Mindful of the currency market consequences, Major decided to press on with UK ratification. Lamont blamed the prime minister for missing a chance to derail Maastricht. Major's analysis, 15 years later, was that he had no choice but to deal with a 'concatenation of events. The Danish No led to a French decision on a referendum. This in turn led to the possibility of the death of the Maastricht treaty, and a halt to European integration – which would have caused a bloodbath on a mega-scale on the financial markets.'[3]

The Danish vote exposed fundamental European fractures over the road to a single currency. On the one side were those, like French Prime Minister Pierre Bérégovoy, who saw Maastricht as a means to escape from 'the Europe of blood and fire' and 'erase centuries of fratricidal strife'.[4] Bérégovoy warned that non-ratification of Maastricht could 'break up' Europe: 'Germany, which is today integrated into Europe… could be free to follow its own will.'[5] On the other were those who were deeply worried about the dire economics behind the Maastricht structures. Many UK economists were warning that, with Britain in recession, the government had joined the ERM at too high a rate. Sir Donald MacDougall, former government chief economic adviser, wrote in March 1992, 'I favoured entry into the ERM. But when we did so at DM2.95, I feared we were repeating the mistake of 1925, when we returned to the gold standard at too high a rate. Events since we entered have convinced me I was right, and that we need to devalue.'[6]

European governments' difficulties in carrying the people to some form of unity were manifest. The Danes – who eventually joined the UK by negotiating an 'opt-out' from the treaty commitment to monetary union – paved the way for a quarter of a century of skirmishes over member states' flexibility in setting the European Community's future. In what turned out to be an accurate post-Danish referendum depiction of a 'more fluid structure' for Europe's future, the *Financial Times* described on 4 June 1992 how 'progress towards a more united Europe would occur through irregular shifts, with the different countries maintaining freedom to decide which of several concentric circles they wished to join.'[7]

Fault lines were already well discernible. Just 10 days before the Denmark shock, Britain's prime minister clashed with his predecessor over the democratic impact of the Maastricht journey. John Major rejected any idea that Europe was heading towards a 'super-state', affirming that the European treaty 'marks the point at which, for the first time, we have begun to reverse that centralising trend.' Thatcher on the other hand declared that Maastricht 'passes colossal powers from parliamentary governments to a centralised bureaucracy.'[8] Klaus Kinkel, the German foreign minister, describing himself as the 'foster son' of his predecessor Hans-Dietrich Genscher, emphasised that the European Union was 'even more important' for reunified Germany: 'The European path is absolutely without alternative.'[9] This jarred with a public display of German anti-EMU antipathy with the release of a manifesto from more than 60 leading German economists pointing to the dangers for the monetary union plan posed by lack of economic convergence and democratic legitimacy.[10]

After the Danish rejection, the foreign exchanges turned against the lira as 'the weakest link in the chain'. This reflected weakness in the Italian economy and long-standing foreign exchange market doubts whether Italy was competitive at its ERM exchange rate against a D-mark that was climbing rapidly against the dollar.[11] The mainstream European reaction was to plough on regardless. French Treasury Director Jean-Claude Trichet – later governor of the Banque de France and president of the European Central Bank – told the European Monetary Committee, a day after the Danish vote, that the other 11 Community states should proceed without the Danes. Denmark 'should be punished for its foolishness'.[12] This led to a clash with Wolfgang Rieke, the head of the Bundesbank's international department, who described the No vote as 'a well-timed reminder'. Rieke commented on 'Trichet's arrogance in arguing that it is outrageous that "the people" (of an insignificant country) should be allowed to derail these grand plans'. The Bank of England's Andrew Crockett saw the vote as 'a major setback' but also 'a useful warning to the "dirigiste types" (the French)'. Rieke pointed out German disquiet about the EMU process. Latest opinion polls in Germany were 90% to 10% against giving up the D-mark and 80% to 20% against Maastricht. The European Commission had to reprint its German language text of the Maastricht treaty because it referred to 'Ecu' (for European Unit of Account) as a word. The Bonn government insisted that 'ECU' was merely an acronym and not the agreed name for the planned single currency.

Economist Peter Spencer summed up Britain's predicament: 'Just before we joined the ERM, the Berlin wall came down, landing Germany's federal government with a big bill, which it decided for political reasons to finance by borrowing, pushing up real interest rates on the continent.' The result was 'an Anglo-Saxon debt mountain, which is a hangover from Shadow ERM and the Lawson boom, and German-style real interest rates, a consequence of ERM membership and developments in Germany'.[13] Setting the tone for many furious controversies over Bundesbank policies, Schlesinger apologised to the British ambassador over a press report that the Bundesbank advocated an ERM realignment.[14] Finance Minister Theo Waigel visited the Bundesbank in June 1992 and urged the central bank to hold firm.[15]

After the Federal Reserve cut its discount rate to 3%, the lowest for 30 years, alarm bells started to sound in London. Norman Lamont was feeling 'increasingly trapped by the ERM', but had no alternative but to continue mounting the public case for adhesion, including in a speech to the European Policy Forum on 11 July. The result of any alternative to the current monetary policy would be 'higher interest rates, higher inflation or, most likely, both.'[16] The solution to the UK's predicament had to come, the British government believed, from Germany. In the first of three extraordinary letters of protest over German monetary policy, Major wrote to Kohl on 14 July: 'I am very concerned about the effect of any further increase in interest rates in Europe.' He criticised 'reports emanating from the Bundesbank' that countries unhappy with their ERM parities should devalue. The prime minister asked Kohl to tell Schlesinger at the Bundesbank 'how damaging such stories are'.[17] Kohl did not reply, but the Bundesbank's answer came, Major wrote, 'from the barrel of a gun': its 10th successive increase in the discount rate, to 8.75%, the highest since 1931.

At the Bundesbank meeting on 16 July that decided the move, Jürgen Möllemann, the economics minister, warned that the central bank was drifting into international turbulence. At the G7 economic summit in Munich 10 days earlier, government leaders of all participating countries except Italy had criticised Germany's interest rate stance.[18] Further tightening could damage sentiment in east Germany, where a 'political time bomb was ticking', as well as internationally. The Bundesbank's international credibility 'would not suffer', Möllemann claimed, if the central bank refrained from raising rates – advice that Schlesinger, pointing to rising inflation in both the east and west of the country, politely advised his colleagues to ignore. Commenting on the German rate rise, Bérégovoy told the French Cabinet in Paris on 22 July how, in the future, everything could change for the better: 'If a common central bank existed for the 12 states of the Community, then a decision such as the one the Bundesbank has just taken would not be possible.'[19]

CHAPTER FOURTEEN

Hint of sabotage

The drumbeat of disquiet about Britain's commitment to its D-mark link echoed loudly in Frankfurt. Hans Tietmeyer, the Bundesbank deputy president, told successive Bundesbank council meetings on 6 and 20 August 1992 of continuing public discussion in Britain about 'a realignment or departure from the ERM'.[1] Tietmeyer reported at the second gathering that the Bundesbank and other central banks had sold DM7bn in the fortnight since 6 August to try to depress the D-mark against weaker currencies, above all sterling and the lira. Helmut Schlesinger delivered a somewhat unnecessary reminder that the Bundesbank would remain wedded to the goal of reducing inflation to '2% or less'. He told his colleagues of the need for 'restraint in public statements to reduce nervousness on markets', a prescient if somewhat ironic forewarning of later turbulence his unguarded comments were to unleash.

In mid-August the Bank of England – in an internal paper that bore the hallmarks of Deputy Governor Eddie George – sought to reassure the Treasury on the underlying strength of the UK's foreign exchange reserves.[2] Norman Lamont's tentative efforts, discussed with Sarah Hogg, one of Major's key aides, to persuade the prime minister of the merits of suspending ERM membership came to nothing. Much to Lamont's annoyance, in a meeting called to broach the subject, Major declined to discuss it.[3]

Advice from continental economists was mixed. André Szász, a senior official at the Nederlandsche Bank in Amsterdam, a veteran of decades of European monetary tangles, recommended the British government to stick to its guns. Experience showed that 'devaluation ends up increasing interest rates rather than lowering them'. Ernst-Moritz Lipp, chief economist at Dresdner Bank in Frankfurt, however, correctly foresaw pressures building towards an autumn upheaval. He suggested Britain should join forces with France to persuade the Germans to revalue the D-mark. If that failed, Britain should 'decouple' from the D-mark and devalue unilaterally as a legitimate reaction to the extreme monetary pressures of German unification.[4]

The foreign exchange market's growing scepticism about the ability of governments and central banks to impose their will was reinforced by a currency market showdown on 21 August. The dollar had fallen 20% in the previous year and the US administration felt the time had come for a reversal, as had been accomplished in 1985 through the Plaza agreement and 1987 through the Louvre accord.[5]

This time the US Treasury orchestrated coordinated support-buying of dollars by 18 central banks in the thin holiday market to turn around the direction of the dollar. But the scale of buying was insufficient to convince the market of the 'real resolve' of the authorities and the exercise 'back-fired'.[6] 'Yesterday's action raises questions about the credibility of internationally coordinated exchange rate policy,' observed the *Financial Times*, calling the intervention 'disastrous'. 'The importance of the intervention on 21 August was that it failed,' observed Lamont, 'It demonstrated to the markets just how powerless central banks really were and paved the way for later events.'[7]

To deal with the rising tension, finance ministers and central bankers from France, Germany, Britain and Italy convened in Paris on 26 August. Before setting off, Norman Lamont formally announced he wanted to remove 'any scintilla of doubt' about the UK's ERM commitment. This was followed by overt intervention from the Bank of England to shore up sterling.[8] The effect was undone when Reimut Jochimsen, a well-known Maastricht sceptic on the Bundesbank council, pointed publicly to 'potential for realignment' within the ERM – creating a fresh wave of sterling selling.[9]

Just before the meeting, Mitterrand told Kohl on the North Sea island of Borkum, 'I have received some desperate phone calls from Major.'[10] Hints that the Bundesbank was mounting conspiracy against the Maastricht treaty gained ground. A front-page story in *Der Spiegel*, the German news magazine, alleged 'sabotage against Bonn'. In a polemical article in *The Times* urging the benefits of other central banks 'intervening aggressively against the mark', Anatole Kaletsky, the British economist and pundit, castigated the German central bank as 'a political loose cannon and a source of instability not only for European and trans-Atlantic relations, but also for Germany's domestic economic affairs.'[11]

A fog of confusion and helplessness descended over the finance ministers' meeting in Paris. Determined to maintain secrecy, the French authorities insisted on picking up Lamont in a small boat at the Place de la Concorde in the centre of Paris and ferrying him eastwards to a small entrance directly on the river bank at the finance ministry's beetling headquarters at Bercy.[12] According to Bundesbank Deputy President Tietmeyer (standing in for Schlesinger, who was on holiday), 'The other finance ministers came with a message wanting a cut in German interest rates. I said this was out of the question, but I added that I could imagine, from a personal point of view, that Germany could be ready for a unilateral revaluation for the D-mark... However, the other finance ministers rejected this. They didn't want to discuss currency adjustments, only interest rates.'[13]

France was adamant it would maintain the D-mark link. Britain did not want to devalue alone (or with the Italians). Lamont explained, 'If we had devalued, we would have continued in the ERM and would have paid an interest rate penalty... We tried to put together a statement that German rates would go no higher... But Tietmeyer was very difficult and Waigel not helpful.'[14]

The failure of the Paris meeting to break through the ERM impasse intensified a belief in the British Treasury that some form of shake-up was on the way. Jeremy Heywood, Lamont's principal private secretary – destined for a steep ascent in the civil service that saw him become the chief aide to Prime Ministers Tony Blair, Gordon Brown and David Cameron and then Cabinet Secretary from 2012 onwards – was among those closest to the chancellor's forebodings. But he was still considering conventional escape routes out of Britain's impasse.

In a four-page note to Lamont headed 'Contingency measures' on 27 August, Heywood broached the possibility of an interest rate rise but suggested that Lamont could use the Conservative party conference in early October – 'we can (just about) wait' – to announce a range of measures to help the housing market, possibly mobilising as much as £1bn, as 'the most effective way of spending cash in 1992-93'.[15] A large part of the possible package could be a highly politically motivated £700m for 'off the shelf purchases by housing associations, buying roughly 15,000 properties slanted as a far as possible to the South East.'

After the Paris session Major telephoned Kohl to browbeat him again on the Bundesbank and called Giuliano Amato, the Italian prime minister, to urge him to do the same.[16] Amato was increasingly worried about pressure on the lira and other weaker currencies. Four days after the finance ministers' meeting, he flew to Paris to ask Bérégovoy to explore whether France could join in a general ERM realignment. The French prime minister said he understood Italy's plight but could do nothing to help as franc weakness would reduce the chances of a Yes in the Maastricht referendum. Amato told him the lira could probably not hold out for that long.[17] Major had meanwhile written again to Kohl saying the Bundesbank had to choose 'between a cut in interest rates in Germany and an increase in rates across all Europe… I urged him to tell the Bundesbank council that higher interest rates risked turning the recession into a slump.'[18] At the end of August, Major wrote to Kohl for the third time. 'German reunification is at the heart of these problems… Britain strongly supported [this] but many in Britain believe they are now having to pay a high price… The attitude adopted by the Bundesbank… is difficult to understand.'[19]

Major's letter at last produced an effect, but it was not the one the prime minister desired. He received a reply a few days later after Downing Street asked Christopher Mallaby, the British ambassador to Germany, to intervene. 'Helmut wrote, "The Bundesbank does not intend to further increase interest rates" – which was welcome as far as it went, but ignored the reality that reductions were urgently needed.'[20]

Stung into action, Kohl summoned his monetary helmsmen to the Bonn chancellery on 2 September to work out a common Bonn-Frankfurt policy – effectively healing months of disputes between the Bundesbank and the government. 'The Major letters were totally counterproductive,' Waigel explained in 2007. 'This brought the two sides together.'[21] Tietmeyer commented that Major's action in trying to influence the Bundesbank via Bonn was particularly flawed – although similar pressure applied by President Mitterrand later was more successful.[22] Later, Major robustly defended his tactics: 'There was no point in discussing a detailed economic point with Helmut on the telephone… If I had asked the governor of the

Bank of England to write to the Bundesbank, this would have had less clout. If I had dispatched a "round robin" letter signed by Amato, Bérégovoy and myself, there would have been the danger of a leak which would have caused turmoil on the markets.'[23]

In a 1 September telephone conference between European central banks the French, Italian and British representatives called for further European intervention to support the dollar to protect their currencies within the ERM against a strengthening D-mark – a policy the Bundesbank regarded with intense scepticism.[24] Schlesinger's message, repeated several times in cryptic public statements, was 'we are not in a [European] monetary union', a coded invitation to other countries to decide a realignment, but one that France, in particular, because of the imminence of the Maastricht referendum, was unwilling to accept.[25]

On 3 September Major telephoned Amato again – 'a worried man'.[26] On the same day Tietmeyer told the Bundesbank council that the finance ministers' statement after the Paris meetings ruling out an ERM realignment had 'led to only a negligible relaxation of tension on the markets'.[27] He reported record D-mark sales – DM22.7bn since 20 August, and DM8.6bn by the Bank of England since 28 July – to prop up weaker currencies. Schlesinger told the Bundesbank meeting that high wage increases in Germany in the febrile post-reunification environment 'had worsened the position for monetary policy'. However, 'a realignment was not under political discussion – we will have to wait for developments.'

The next day European finance ministers and central bank governors gathered at the spa town of Bath in southwest England for an ill-tempered two-day meeting. Italy raised its key interest rate to 15%. The British government announced an Ecu10bn international bank loan to defend sterling, a sign of defiance, as well as misplaced confidence. UK ministers and officials did not realise that New York hedge fund manager George Soros was simultaneously amassing borrowing lines of $10bn to bet against sterling – and that, armed with considerably greater insights into the Bundesbank's philosophy and tactics (partly through having observed Helmut Schlesinger's scepticism about supporting sterling at an investment conference in Frankfurt a few weeks earlier), Soros had a good chance of winning the scrimmage.

Italian Prime Minister Amato had been considering a similar 'jumbo loan' for Italy – but turned down the idea since, if his country had to devalue against other European currencies, repaying the loan would be prodigiously expensive.

The disagreement which had dogged Europe for weeks – the Germans wanted a realignment, the others, a cut in German interest rates – came to the surface with renewed ferocity. Lamont, chairing the Bath meeting, repeatedly asked Schlesinger to cut rates. Like many others before him, he appeared oblivious of the Bundesbank's legendary stubbornness. As Wim Duisenberg, the former Nederlandsche Bank president, once said, 'The Bundesbank is like whipped cream – the more you beat it, the harder it becomes.' Increasingly impatiently, Schlesinger said 'No'[28] – gesturing at one point (restrained by Waigel, the German finance minister) to walk out of the meeting – an empty threat, since there was no transport to take him away from the elegant surroundings of the Royal Crescent Hotel. All the Germans would do was to undertake not to raise rates 'in present circumstances', according to a somewhat mealy-mouthed closing statement.

'Everyone in Europe saw a fall in German interest rates as the solution to the economic tensions,' said Leigh-Pemberton.[29] 'The Germans' position at Bath was obstinately resolute. They were egging each other on to stand fast. They knew a crisis was coming up,' Dutch Finance Minister Wim Kok recalled, 'Everyone dug in their heels.'[30] Schlesinger's stately and gregarious wife Carola, with him in Bath, an old acquaintance of Britain's Denis Healey, told friends afterwards that no one had ever before been so rude to her husband.[31]

According to Lamont, 'I had to ask for interest rates to fall. I was aware of the Bundesbank's independence and that the move might be counter-productive, but it was our last resort. I was speaking on behalf of others too – the French, the Italians, the Irish. They all asked me as chairman to make the points I did.'[32] Lamont's successor Kenneth Clarke later criticised British tactics: 'There was a ludicrous assumption that, if things got difficult, the Germans would bail us out. However, Kohl was not interested in economics. He was always very respectful of the economic judgement of Schlesinger and Tietmeyer at the Bundesbank.'[33]

Speaking diplomatically at the end of the meeting, Lamont said, 'One of the questions raised was whether the very special and unique circumstances of reunification in Germany are now not acting through monetary policy as a drag on Europe.'[34] The Bath meeting was followed by fresh currency attrition, focused at first on the Nordic currencies. Sweden, which was not in the ERM but kept the krona pegged to European currencies, implemented drastic monetary tightening that subsequently pushed overnight lending rates to an astronomical 500%. The Finnish markka was floated and fell 14% against the ECU.

Pressure mounted on the lira. Italy, not Britain, appeared in the eye of the storm. The Banca d'Italia's Lamberto Dini said: 'During the crisis period in September 1992, we had an outflow of reserves of $40bn to $50bn. Everyone underestimated the strength of capital flows.'[35] Despite the storm clouds, in a dinner speech to Scottish industrialists on 10 September, Major anchored his policies firmly to the ERM. In advance of the prime minister's speech William Morris, minister of Glasgow cathedral, delivered what Major said was 'a novel Grace':

Each use restraint, reduce inflation
To be a slimmer, fitter nation
And not be sunk in deep depression
When waist and hairlines face recession
Oh Lord, Thou dost with steady interest wait
Which of Thy family will devaluate.

The prime minister told his audience Britain had controlled costs in the ERM and boosted exports and productivity to record levels. Problems were caused by the weakness of the dollar, which had fallen by more than 20% against the D-mark, but the country would not be blown off course. 'I was under no illusions when I took Britain into the ERM. I said at the time that membership was no soft option. The soft option, the devaluer's option, the inflationary option, in my judgement that would be a betrayal of our future.' To applause, the prime minister added, 'I tell you categorically, that is not the government's policy.'[36]

Six days

CHAPTER FIFTEEN

Weekend manoeuverings

John Major's verbal defence of the sterling exchange rate was no mere rhetorical flourish. The prime minister was deeply convinced of the rightness of his actions. Yet his resistance was futile, as a weekend of elaborate manoeuvring was to demonstrate. *The Times* wrote in a caustic editorial on Friday 11 September, 'The currency markets do not seem to believe him. If they did, sterling would not be floundering at the bottom of the ERM… Why are international investors treating Mr Major's promises with the respect due to a used-car salesman? The reason is simple. Mr Major can no more guarantee to maintain an arbitrary price for sterling in the market place than could his benighted predecessor in the 1950s and 1960s.'[1] *The Times* editorial marked the beginning of the 'hot phase' of sterling attrition. Major was about to become the latest prime minister – after Anthony Eden, Harold Wilson, Edward Heath and James Callaghan – in a long litany of British failure in jousting with currency speculators.

Far more than the political leadership of the UK was at stake. On Friday morning – a day after the Italian central bank publicly complained about 'excessively high' German interest rates[2] – the Bundesbank and Banca d'Italia became embroiled in a deep-seated financial controversy that went to the heart of the rules governing the European Monetary System. On Friday morning, the lira fell to its lowest permitted ERM point, triggering obligatory intervention from both central banks.[3] In the light of massive inflows of liquidity threatening to disrupt the German money supply, the Bundesbank invoked a shadowy document from 1978 under which the central bank could ask the government to free it from the constraint of making unlimited support purchases of weak European currencies.

The stipulation had been forced on the German government at the birth of the EMS 14 years earlier. In November 1978 Otmar Emminger, the Bundesbank president, sent Chancellor Helmut Schmidt his approval of key elements of the prospective EMS agreement coupled with a list of points for further clarification. They included the need to safeguard the Bundesbank's 'autonomy' and its desire to be freed from the obligation to intervene with unlimited support for weaker currencies at times of monetary crisis.[4] In a series of opaque manoeuvres Schmidt agreed to the Bundesbank's strictures – a notable concession by a politician who later tried to pretend that the EMS resulted from his own coercion of the Bundesbank, rather than from his agreement to the Bundesbank's 'stability-first' conditions. During an extraordinary visit to the Bundesbank on 30 November 1978 in which Schmidt praised 'the unusual utility' of the Bundesbank's arguments, the chancellor emphasised his 'factual agreement' with freeing the Bundesbank from the obligation to make unlimited intervention purchases, heavily weakening the automatic nature of Bundesbank support for weaker currencies. He insisted the accord should never be allowed to get into French or Italian newspapers, telling the Bundesbank council, in words that were never officially published, 'The editorials would criticise their own governments for believing such a shallow promise from the Germans.'[5]

The Bundesbank's opt-out from the obligation to support ERM currencies had never been a complete secret. News had leaked out in Germany at the end of 1978, notably in a report in *Handelsblatt*,[6] but the Germans had no interest in spreading the message to the other ERM countries. On 11 September the Italians were the first to hear that reality was harsher than it had previously appeared. Sometimes conversations between the Italians and their German counterparties could verge on the haphazard. On one occasion the Bonn chancellery received a phone call on a Saturday morning. Alerted by the switchboard, Kohl's officials reported, 'Someone's on the telephone and wants to speak to the chancellor, he sounds Italian.' The caller turned out to be Carlo Azeglio Ciampi, governor of the Banca d'Italia, who was later put through to Theo Waigel, the finance minister, at Munich airport.[7]

On 11 September, the interlocutor was again Ciampi, conferring with Giuliano Amato, the prime minister, and Piero Barucci, the finance minister, at Amato's office at the Palazzo Chigi in Rome when Ciampi was called to the telephone to be told the Bundesbank would stop intervening to support the lira on Monday. Amato recalled:

> There was a knock at the door of my office. The Bundesbank was on the line and the call had been put through to the palazzo. He went out to speak with the Bundesbank president at the place where my secretary sits. When he came back after 15 to 20 minutes his face was white, turning to green. The Germans were explaining what was, to us, a surprising refusal to offer D-marks to the markets. We thought there was an obligation under the existing agreement. But this turned out not to be the case. Schlesinger told Ciampi that, at the time when the EMS agreement was signed, the Bundesbank had secured an agreement from Chancellor Schmidt. This laid down that, irrespective of what the government had undertaken, the Bundesbank preserved its responsibility to safeguard the stability of the D-mark and suspend sales of D-marks if this was thought to be exaggeratedly swelling the money supply.[8]

After a day of rearguard currency action, the evening of 11 September saw another dramatic Bundesbank visit. Helmut Kohl, Theo Waigel, Horst Köhler, state secretary in the finance ministry, Gert Haller, head of the ministry's international department, and Johannes Ludewig, head of the chancellor's economics team, conferred with Schlesinger and Tietmeyer at the Bundesbank's squat guesthouse in the grounds of its Frankfurt headquarters.[9] Currency decisions are formally issues for the government, not the central bank, and the Bundesbank put forward its request that the government seek a realignment by Germany's monetary partners.[10] 'The message from the government,' Tietmeyer said, 'was that they were ready for a D-mark revaluation, while Schlesinger indicated that, in this case, a German interest rate cut would be possible. It was decided that Köhler and I would travel the following day first to Paris and then to Rome.'[11]

The key interlocutor in Paris was Jean-Claude Trichet, the French Treasury director and chairman of the European Monetary Committee, in charge of European realignment procedures. The Rome journey was necessary to win the support of the Italians that the lira would be devalued as part of the package. Schlesinger recalled, 'The order to Köhler and Tietmeyer was that they were to seek to carry out as broad realignment as possible,' involving a formal lowering of the ERM currency values of the four weakest currencies, the lira, sterling, Spanish peseta and Portuguese escudo. Schlesinger told Kohl and the others at the Friday evening Bundesbank meeting: 'The stronger and wider the realignment, the more I will be able to ask for a cut in interest rates at the Bundesbank council.'[12]

Leading Germans proclaimed afterwards that they believed, erroneously, that – after the preliminary discussions with Köhler and Tietmeyer – Trichet would convene a full-scale European realignment meeting on Sunday in Brussels. Schlesinger said, 'Late on Saturday evening [12 September], when Tietmeyer and Köhler returned from Paris and Rome, and even on Sunday morning, when Tietmeyer telephoned me at my home, I still believed there would be a monetary committee meeting in Brussels. When Tietmeyer phoned me, I believed he was calling from Brussels; in fact he was telephoning from his home. So a broad realignment did not take place.'

The reality is, in their conversations with other countries that weekend, the German monetary authorities did not press for a full-scale meeting of the monetary committee. Only a week before the potential upheaval of the Maastricht referendum, France never had any intention to hold a physical meeting. The Germans complied with this view, believing the risks of a full-scale realignment outweighed the advantages. Michel Sapin, the French finance minister, explained:

> We [the government] were obsessed by the Maastricht referendum on 20 September. We were convinced that Maastricht was indispensable for the creation of the new Europe. If we created additional tensions on the foreign exchange markets, there would be a greater risk that the referendum would end in a No. At the meeting with the Germans [on 12 September], everyone was ambiguous. We were playing for a calm outcome. We French were certain in our minds that we did not want to have a full meeting of the European Monetary Committee, but we did not express this clearly. The Germans were trying to test whether there was an opportunity for a full EMS realignment, in exchange for a larger cut in German interest rates, but they also did not express themselves clearly.[13]

Theo Waigel, the German finance minister, concurred with France's reasoning. 'They had kept the rate stable against Germany for many years, even at the cost of high interest rates. They were proud of this achievement. A devaluation would have been a catastrophe. Maintaining the franc rate had become part of the central doctrine of the French state.'[14]

The Rome talks with the two German emissaries on Saturday afternoon were more clear-cut. By invoking the Emminger letter, Germany forced Italy's hand. Tietmeyer told his Italian hosts, led by Finance Minister Barucci, 'There's no way we can support the lira anymore.'[15] Italy agreed to devalue the lira that weekend. But the agreement was reached in a telephone conference of the monetary committee, rather than in a full-scale meeting, and no other European currencies were involved, leaving many ERM members overvalued against the D-mark. Crucially, the Germans did not communicate to the UK over the crucial weekend any suggestion that a wider realignment would have brought deeper cuts in Bundesbank interest rates. According to Lamont, Eddie George spoke to Tietmeyer on Sunday 13 September, but there was no mention of a wider realignment or any interest rate benefits this would bring.[16] Barucci recalled how Köhler and Tietmeyer in the Rome meeting 'maintained that the German economy was booming. In order to avoid inflation, they could not further reduce their interest rates.'[17]

In view of the Germans' over-confidence in the strength of their economy, there are doubts about the credibility of Bundesbank protestations in the years following the 1992 episodes that, if the realignment had been wider and deeper, the Bundesbank council would have immediately cut interest rates more substantially. The unfolding events of September 1992 – the withdrawal of sterling and the lira from the ERM and the subsequent devaluations of the peseta, escudo and Irish pound – generated a much larger appreciation of the D-mark against the weaker currencies than would have ensued from the 'wider realignment' the Bundesbank said it wanted on 11 September. Nonetheless, following the September cuts in discount and Lombard rates, the Bundesbank kept interest rates on hold, much to France's disappointment. Schlesinger proved obstinate in rejecting further significant easing during the rest of his time in office up to 1993.

News of the impending lira devaluation reached London on Saturday evening. Terry Burns, permanent secretary of the Treasury, learned of the development via a phone call from Nigel Wicks, his second-in-command, while attending a wedding anniversary party in a school sports pavilion in southeast London. Lamont was told later that evening after returning from the Last Night of the Proms at the Royal Albert Hall.[18] Lamont met at the Treasury with leading officials at 7.30am on Sunday, who heard that Trichet would handle the impending Italian currency change without a full-scale meeting. The option of whether Britain should join the Italians was briefly mentioned but was not the subject of any discussion. Trichet did not approach the British with any offer of a full-scale realignment. If he had done so, it is evident he would have been rebuffed.

John Major made clear that, over the weekend, no wider ERM change was ever broached, since neither France nor Britain wanted it. 'If we had tried to press for a general realignment, with sterling and the French franc moving down together, then the French would have flipped – it would have cut them off at the knees. We wouldn't have got the realignment that we needed. There would have been a huge row and no outcome. This might have led to the French voting No in the referendum. That would have led to the wrecking of the Maastricht treaty. And the other Europeans would have blamed perfidious Albion. No doubt Jean-Claude Trichet saw things the same way that we did. And that's why he did not call a realignment meeting.'[19]

Against this background, Italian efforts to cajole Britain into a wider realignment were doomed from the start. Following a brief conversation between Lamont and Barucci, Amato spoke to Major on the telephone at 9.45am on Sunday, while the British prime minister was staying with the Queen at the Scottish castle of Balmoral. Major had to stick a finger in one ear to drown out a piper walking on the lawn outside playing a lament.[20] 'I wanted to convince him to take part in a general realignment,' Amato said. 'He said sterling would not take part in the operation. I asked him if sterling would still be stable after the Italian realignment. He said, "Yes, we feel safe."'[21] Amato concluded the conversation by saying Italy would have to go it alone with a new parity. When Major told him 'Good luck, Giuliano,' Amato countered, darkly, 'I should say good luck, John.'[22] Up until the Amato-Major call, an Italian government aircraft had been kept on standby to take Mario Draghi, the Italian Treasury director (later governor of the Banca d'Italia and then president of the ECB), to a Brussels meeting of the European Monetary Committee. Afterwards the aircraft was stood down. Fabrizio Saccomanni of the Banca d'Italia said, 'It was a terrible thing that weekend. We were left isolated... The British attitude was, "We can handle that." They said they had recently contracted large loans on the international markets. They had plenty of reserves. I told the Bank of England, "This is going to be a very difficult moment for all of us." But the Bank did not consider that this danger was real.[23]

In contrast to the government's misplaced confidence, the dire tone on 13 September of Britain's Sunday newspapers struck a much truer note. David Smith, in the *Sunday Times*, wrote that the government's strategy was 'to hang on grimly' until German interest rates started to fall at the end of the year. 'But the end of the year, to the financial markets, is an eternity away. Europe, already facing a bleak economic prospect, is entering its most critical phase. Sweden and Italy are experiencing the full horrors of Europe's monetary madness. Others will suffer too.'[24] Andrew Marshall in the *Independent on Sunday* harked back to Irish poet W.B. Yeats' *The Second Coming*, written in 1919: 'Things fall apart; the centre cannot hold; Mere anarchy is loosed upon the world'. Looking presciently a quarter of a century ahead, Marshall saw that Europe was approaching a watershed.

> The vision that Yeats sketched out, painful, pessimistic and atavistic, was of a world where older demons come back to haunt us. It is a vision that seems suddenly and unexpectedly to have returned to western Europe... Maastricht is under fire from all sides. The right in every country rejects it. The target of the French No campaign is what they call technocracy, the denial of citizenship that the EC's distant bureaucratic structures seem to represent. But the consequences of bringing down borders are also the target: the rise of immigration, fears of crime spreading across frontiers, of the loss of the control that nation-states painstakingly assembled over centuries.... Britain might want the EC to be only a free-trade area; but that is not what the rest of the continent wants. Indeed, the wind is blowing against freer trade. The EC is supposed to be a bulwark against those older forces, a sea-wall against storms. If it does not fulfil that function, western Europe will find something else that does. The centre may hold: but Britain may not be there.[25]

CHAPTER SIXTEEN

Schlesinger's message

The Bundesbank council met in Frankfurt at 9.30am on Monday morning 14 September to decide a cut in interest rates. The move, prepared by President Helmut Schlesinger in telephone calls with his central bank colleagues on Sunday, and announced prematurely by Theo Waigel, the self-assured German finance minister, in a radio interview on Sunday evening, resulted in an unspectacular 0.25 percentage point cut in the internationally-significant Lombard rate and a 0.5 point cut in the discount and money market rates. This was the first Bundesbank credit easing for nearly five years. The widespread perception that the interest rate cut had been orchestrated by politicians vexed the Bundesbank. German newspapers had been carrying stories highlighting French President Mitterrand's view that future European central bank officials would be no more than 'technicians' carrying out government orders.[1] On Sunday Michel Sapin, Mitterrand's finance minister, gave advance praise to the Bundesbank's rate cut as a sign of 'solidarity' in Europe paving the way for fresh interest rate reductions 'necessary to support growth and employment'.[2] Unknown to most observers, there had been a highly relevant precedent for successful pressure on the supposedly politically unmovable Bundesbank to accede to governmental wishes. The previous Bundesbank discount rate cut – a 0.5 percentage point fall to 2.5% decided in December 1987 – had taken place after a telephone call from Chancellor Helmut Kohl requesting action from Karl Otto Pöhl to help shore up world financial markets.[3]

The relatively modest cut in German interest rates, and the events leading up to it, unleashed three sets of consequences, all of them destabilising for sterling. First, Britain's refusal even to countenance joining the lira in a devaluation, grounded in the belief that sterling's ERM parity was justified, left it vulnerable to attack – especially as the Bundesbank made its own view plain in coming days that the pound was over-valued. Second, after some initial optimism, the financial markets were unimpressed by the Bundesbank's interest rate move, which did not go far enough to assuage dealers' concerns that the Germans were still on a diametrically different monetary policy course to the one required by most of their partners. Third, and most significant, pre-announcement of the credit easing by Waigel and Sapin – and the implication that the politicians were now running Germany's monetary policies – steeled Schlesinger for a bout of muscle-flexing. The challenge to the Bundesbank's authority intensified Schlesinger's resolve to have the last word on a crucial question of who oversaw Germany's monetary policy: the central bank or the politicians. Over the next two days, through a string of largely haphazard circumstances, Schlesinger's message would hurtle around the world.

At the head of the Bundesbank's 13th floor council table, Schlesinger summarised for the other 15 members the dramatic conversations with the German government on Friday 14 September. He recounted, too, Saturday's emergency visits by Tietmeyer and Köhler to Paris and Rome.[4] The Bundesbank had been forced to buy DM23.6bn worth of lira at the lower ERM intervention point, Schlesinger reported, injecting massive volumes of liquidity into the German banking system with potentially inflationary effects on the German money supply. 'The Italians wished to wait until after the French referendum on 20 September before reacting [to the currency weakness],' he said. 'This would not be acceptable for the Bundesbank, since there was a likelihood of massive new inflows before this date.' The Bundesbank had made it known over the weekend it would be prepared to accompany a realignment with a cut in interest rates, with the size of the credit easing dependent on the scope of the currency change.

Tietmeyer told the meeting that, in the weekend talks, both France and Italy had 'initially strongly rejected' any parity changes. Sapin had told his German visitors a realignment could prejudice the referendum result. 'Only after long negotiations did France declare itself willing not to oppose an Italian [realignment] initiative.' Italy saw the 'great risks associated with further ERM tensions' and agreed to a 7% devaluation 'only after difficult discussions'. Britain 'as expected' had refused to devalue the pound, Tietmeyer reported, and the Spanish government followed the UK lead by ruling out lowering the peseta's value. According to the official transcript of the Bundesbank proceedings, Schlesinger told the meeting a realignment which went further would have been preferable, but the weekend solution was still better than maintaining the present parities. 'In view of the situation on the foreign exchange markets, [Schlesinger] asked council members to exercise restraint in critical public statements on the agreed solution' – a stricture to which the president himself, with striking results, conspicuously failed to adhere. In the press conference after the council meeting, Schlesinger made clear the Bundesbank's reluctance to decide the interest rate cut, which he said 'was not easy for us' in view of 'considerable' German inflation. He added meaningfully that many European partners believed the ERM was already a 'currency union rather than a system of fixed but adjustable exchange rates', but gave no further hints of a preference for further exchange rate changes, pointing out (without mentioning the UK by name) that 'other nations' had large currency reserves partly augmented by borrowing.

Given the degree of flammable tinder strewn across the world economic scene, Schlesinger did his best in the press conference to maintain calm on the currency markets. But as the Bundesbank's true feelings rapidly emerged, his efforts soon turned out to be inadequate. As an ominous sign of the havoc in store, the lira failed to recover on Monday after the weekend devaluation, a change from the usual pattern when currencies rebound after being extensively sold by speculators. Seen from the Bank of England's dealing room, the lack of a substantial Italian rally on 14 September propelled the prospect of a sterling ERM crisis from 'if' to 'when', according to Jim Trott, the Bank's chief dealer. From that point on, sterling's ERM position was 'moving from stress to a car crash'.[5]

Into this disturbed environment on Monday morning strode two British emissaries, Mervyn King and Alan Budd, chief economist of the Bank of England and chief economic adviser to the Treasury, who at around 10.30am visited first the Bundesbank in Frankfurt and then, later that day, the finance ministry in Bonn.[6] The aim of the expeditionary force was to provide the economic justification for the political ebullience shown over the weekend: there would be no question of sterling joining the weaker currencies in any devaluation against the D-mark. The meeting had been suggested a few days earlier by Nigel Wicks, who had gained the impression the previous week from Horst Köhler at the German finance ministry that the Germans had severe doubts about the sterling exchange rate. Feelings of unease were widespread. On 10 September Norman Lamont had prepared a draft letter to Schlesinger – which the Bank of England prevailed upon him not to send – protesting against the effect of 'sources at the Bundesbank… saying that a devaluation of sterling was inevitable.'[7]

On Monday morning Otmar Issing, the Bundesbank's director for economics, received the British tandem, accompanied by Reiner König, Issing's deputy and head of the central bank's economics department. King and Budd had not previously met Issing, strengthening the perception that the British had been remiss in not building personal relationships with their German counterparts. Furthermore, Schlesinger was not informed about the meeting and was unsure whether Leigh-Pemberton knew about it. 'He did not inform me, as was the usual practice between governors,' Schlesinger said later.[8] The meeting showed every sign of an emergency. King interrupted his holiday to fly to Frankfurt. Issing, like Budd and King (who had joined the Treasury and Bank in 1991 and 1990, respectively), had not been long in the job, having been plucked from an academic career at Würzburg university to join the Bundesbank in 1990.

Budd's view, fully in line with Treasury thinking, was that 'the main problem was the level of interest rates. I also thought that if the UK devalued and stayed in the ERM then interest rates would rise.'[9] Budd, who termed the mission 'one of the great wasted journeys', said it was decided the previous evening after the Italian devaluation. 'We saw this as an extremely harmful event for sterling. We were there to explain that the sterling exchange rate was not misaligned and was sustainable… My thoughts were that we had done our best to persuade them on the sustainability of the sterling exchange rate, but we weren't at all sure that we had done so. The question of whether there should have been a wider weekend realignment was not discussed.'

Budd said Issing had been 'perfectly polite' but realised afterwards that Schlesinger's anger over his treatment from Lamont at the Bath meeting 10 days previously 'had left effects… I was told later that Schlesinger had become so angry as a result of Lamont's repeated calls to cut interest rates that he was on the point of leaving the meeting. I was not aware of that at the time.' Issing recalled that the two visitors from London presented a series of charts and statistics backing the view that sterling was fairly priced on exchange markets. 'I was not convinced. I went to my desk and produced my own set of charts indicating that sterling was overvalued by perhaps 20%.'[10]

On Tuesday 15 September Lionel Barber and David Marsh wrote in the *Financial Times*,

> Now that the most pressing source of EMS instability – the weakness of the lira – has been defused, there is a risk that speculative pressure will turn to other vulnerable currencies. Sterling, still jittery yesterday, is the most likely focus of attack… All EC governments are trapped in a vicious circle under which faltering growth drives up budget deficits through reducing tax revenues and increasing social security outlays… The spectacle of the Bundesbank being subject to political arm-twisting could have an important impact on the German debate over the Maastricht Treaty, Chancellor Kohl has declared himself ready to abandon the D-mark in return for European union. Mr Kohl has insisted that the planned single European currency must be run by a European central bank as independent as the Bundesbank. President François Mitterrand outlined a contrasting view 12 days ago by affirming that the European central bank would execute policies laid down by European governments, not the independent 'technicians' on the council. The weekend manoeuvrings, heavily criticised by many commentators in Germany yesterday, are bound to heighten fears that the politicians will run the bank – and that German voters will be swapping the D-mark for inflationary 'Esperanto money'.

The psychologically contorted background helps explain why Schlesinger took the fateful step of going ahead with the interview on Tuesday afternoon with *Handelsblatt* and the *Wall Street Journal* that had earlier been scheduled for the previous Friday, but had been cancelled because of the lira unrest on that day. Schlesinger confirmed later his irritation with Theo Waigel's Sunday evening revelation of the Bundesbank rate cut.[11] Reinstating the cancelled press interview, in spite of agitated markets, would be a way of affirming the Bundesbank's true position above the political fray and putting the record straight. 'Pressure started to rise in the German media that the Bundesbank was somehow under political control with its independence lost. This was the main reason why I agreed to do the interview on Tuesday.'

Schlesinger told the reporters, according to *Handelsblatt* in a message circulated to news agencies on Tuesday evening (using reported speech, rather than direct quotes, but firmly attributed to Schlesinger), and subsequently published in some editions of *Handelsblatt* the following morning,

> It cannot be ruled out that, after the realignment and the German interest rate cut, that one or two currencies could come under pressure before the referendum in France. In a conversation with the *Handelsblatt* and *Wall Street Journal*, he [Schlesinger] commented that the measures taken up to now have, naturally, not definitely resolved the problems. A more comprehensive realignment would have had a greater effect in alleviating EMS tensions. However, in his view, a change in exchange rate parities incorporating other currencies [as well as the lira] was not possible.[12]

'The measured tone of these words belies their extraordinary power,' observed *The Independent*. 'Schlesinger might as well have said: "More EMS currencies are going to have to be devalued this week." Or, in the shorthand of the market: "Sell sterling, lira and pesetas."'[13]

The unorthodox and unscripted provenance of the remarks compounded confusion. He had spoken freely to the two newspapers and had agreed, perhaps somewhat naively, but in line with an institutionalised German tradition in dealing with the press, that they would publish only an approved version of his comments, after first gaining the Bundesbank's 'authorisation'. The *Handelsblatt* editors had sidestepped these strictures by distributing an 'unauthorised' preliminary version of the story in reported speech, 36 hours before Schlesinger's much more innocuous 'authorised' quotes eventually appeared in the newspaper on 17 September. The article, duly sanitised by the Bundesbank, emphasised Schlesinger's view that it had acted autonomously, and not under political pressure, in cutting interest rates on 14 September. Moreover, it highlighted Schlesinger's 'authorised' belief (countering what the *Handelsblatt* story the day before had maintained, but echoing what he had said in the Monday morning press conference) that the UK had sufficient reserves to defend the pound, and that a sterling devaluation was therefore not likely.[14] By then, the 'politically correct' version of Schlesinger's views was no longer relevant. The damage had been done.

Schlesinger had a detailed explanation for the mishap:

The deputy editor of the *Handelsblatt*, whom I knew and had been expecting, didn't come to the Bundesbank for the interview. Instead it was Werner Benkhoff, whom I didn't know, but I could hardly turn him away. Terence Roth from the *Wall Street Journal* behaved correctly. He showed me the quotes two hours later. But Benkhoff from the *Handelsblatt* did not. He released an unauthorised text to the news agencies on the evening of the same day. Benkhoff wrote his article using indirect speech. The news agencies gave prominence to a one-sentence extract saying that I had wished for a larger realignment. This was clearly taken out of context. I couldn't deny what I had actually said. The tape recorders recorded it. Another person might have denied this, but I could not do so.[15]

In London in the early evening of 15 September, as reports came in of Schlesinger's comments, the reaction was explosive. Britain's top monetary officials were meeting with Lamont at the Treasury to discuss a renewed fall in sterling which – even before the Schlesinger interview surfaced – had suffered a bad day. Ian Plenderleith from the Bank of England, attending the meeting with Eddie George, received the news from the Bank's press office and relayed it to the gathering. Mixed with anger was bafflement, 'Schlesie is a friend,' Leigh-Pemberton affirmed. 'He would not have done this to us. If it has happened it must be an accident.'[16] Alan Budd recalled, 'Norman Lamont's immediate reaction was to ask Robin Leigh-Pemberton to contact Schlesinger and ask him to withdraw the remarks. Robin left the room and then came back. Lamont asked him whether he had got hold of Schlesinger. Robin explained that we must understand that this was the president of the Bundesbank and getting him to withdraw such a statement was not all that easy. I thought, "It's all over."'[17]

CHAPTER SEVENTEEN

Swimming against a tidal wave

Wednesday 16 September was a day of transformation for Britain and Europe. Just 12 hours of frenetic foreign exchange trading tore apart Britain's economic strategy. John Major's Conservative government never fully recovered its authority. As Stephen Wall, one of Major's closest aides, said, 'Black Wednesday altered the course of UK policies on Europe, and was fundamentally the end of the Major government.'[1] Britain's new trajectory of EU semi-detachment culminated 24 years later in the referendum vote to leave.

One sizable part of the dynamics of the day came from the power of international capital searching for speculative gains. Pitted against the financial markets were the governmental and monetary authorities in London, Frankfurt and Paris, as they scrambled to gain a semblance of control. It was an unequal struggle. The official world was disunited, and open divergences had emerged among politicians and functionaries in different countries. The markets, on the other hand, were pointing uniformly in just one direction – sell sterling. They were destined to prevail.

Britain's ERM exit in September 1992 was a public, semi-ritualised affair, bound up with widespread political interaction and manoeuvring – an extraordinary contrast to the almost complete lack of consultation that accompanied the act of joining in October 1990. Entering the ERM under Major as chancellor of the exchequer was carried out largely in secret, with no collective Cabinet decision, having been discussed with only a handful of senior ministers and officials. It involved preparing a new system for the exchange rate, and changing the mind of Prime Minister Thatcher, operations too delicate to be carried out with anything other than the greatest discretion. Withdrawal under Major as prime minister was an equally important undertaking – but, this time, it was opened up to outside scrutiny, a result of the all-too-evident conflicts Britain was facing on the exchange markets, with its foreign partners, and in domestic politics. A specific reason for the public nature of the withdrawal process was Major's wish to involve as many senior ministers as possible. The accolades for winning Thatcher's acceptance for joining the ERM could be Major's alone. When the policy ended in failure, Major's natural wish was that responsibility should be collective.

The day started with a display of force. The Bank of England's dealers entered the foreign exchange market conspicuously at around 7.30am. Not long after 8am, Ian Plenderleith, the Bank's head of market operations, held an urgent meeting with Leigh-Pemberton in the governor's office.[2] Plenderleith alerted him that in early trading for every pound the Bank was putting into the market, the market was more than matching it. Leigh-Pemberton telephoned Lamont to give him the first alert of the day that perhaps the line could not be held. Half-an-hour later, with the Bank's intervention heading for $2bn without effect, he called again: 'If we go on like this, we will use up our reserves completely,' the governor warned. 'Devaluation may have to be considered.'[3] In the first 30 minutes of trading the Bank conducted two $600m 'shots' of open intervention while the Bundesbank and Banque de France bought supportively. Sterling rose to DM2.785 but soon fell back to its floor, overwhelmed by the torrent of sterling from New York and Tokyo. They were, the Bank told Lamont, 'staring a base rate increase in the face'.[4] At 8:50am Lamont called Major and told him sterling was under attack and proposed a rate rise. He was 'taken aback' when the prime minister replied that he was 'not keen to do so'.[5]

Lamont was joined by the governor and their advisers at 9am. Leigh-Pemberton reported that the Bank had conducted three rounds of overt intervention, totalling $2bn. Unfortunately the first two had not been very effective 'because a large number of traders had bought sterling out of hours in New York and Tokyo and they had been able simply to turn up and get their money converted at the official rate'.[6] George said the Bank would continue to intervene but the markets were expecting a rate rise that morning. The intervention was 'huge, but it did not make any difference,' an official told *The Sunday Times*. 'We sat and watched sterling on the screens, but it did not budge.'[7] 'They simply find it impossible to comprehend that the weight of money available in the market not only matches, but is greater than that of all of the money of the central banks of the EC put together,' a dealer told the London *Evening Standard*.[8]

At 9am Major chaired a gathering of senior ministers, comprising Douglas Hurd, foreign secretary, Kenneth Clarke, home secretary, Michael Heseltine, trade and industry secretary, and Richard Ryder, chief whip, in the 18th century edifice of Admiralty House overlooking Whitehall. No.10 Downing Street was being refurbished to reinforce its defences against possible terrorist attacks – but the improvised emergency location lacked a telephone switchboard or computer networks. The scheduled subject for discussion was contingency planning for a French No vote in their referendum on Sunday, but ministers were naturally distracted by the stream of reports of the currency crisis.[9] This inner circle was convened by Major twice more during the day, the prime minister thereby wrapping decisions in the cloak of collective responsibility. As Clarke put it, 'We were there to put our hands in the blood.'[10]

The military overtones were pervasive. 'A day of gloom,' Hurd recorded in his diary, 'I crunched across the gravel [to Admiralty House] just as I had done in the same direction during the Cuban missile crisis 30 years earlier. We met in the dining room, with flocked wallpaper and pictures of naval battles, all victories… The laymen present – Ken Clarke, Michael Heseltine, Richard Ryder and myself – found ourselves taking part in the high-pitched climax of a play, at the earlier acts of which we had not been spectators, let alone actors… There was absolutely nothing for us to do.'[11] Another participant spoke of 'quite a cheerful atmosphere, oddly. I suppose it was the spirit of the first world war trenches.'[12] Alan Budd from the Treasury observed: 'I felt as if I knew what it's like to be a German general at the end of the war, with defeat after defeat and people coming into the room with more bad news. The question is then raised: When do you surrender? In a sense it's always too late, because if you had surrendered a day earlier, fewer people would have been killed.'[13] Expressing his frustration at the slow pace of decision-making, Lamont remarked: 'We were bleeding to death, and all we were doing was talking. We had clearly lost the battle, but the generals had refused to recognise it.'[14]

By 10.30am the Bank had already spent $10bn of reserves, to no effect.[15] Lamont spoke again to Major and told him intervention had failed. Sterling was stuck at the intervention rate and the central bank was 'haemorrhaging badly'.[16] This time the prime minister agreed to a rate rise. Leigh-Pemberton held a conference call with his continental counterparts alerting them to the imminent increase and requested help to ease the pressure, hoping for a German rate cut. But Schlesinger said he could do no more than fulfil the Bundesbank's legal obligations.[17] At 11am the Bank of England announced a 2% hike to its minimum lending rate to 12%, accompanied by a statement by Lamont that the government would 'take whatever measures are necessary' to maintain the pound's ERM exchange rate.

The move was sensational. Journalists scurried back to London from the 'torpor' of the Liberal Democrat party conference in Harrogate.[18] Would the market be convinced? The chancellor stood with officials around the desk of his private secretary, Jeremy Heywood, watching the market's reaction on a Reuters screen displaying live prices; nothing happened. Lamont withdrew into his office and 'sat alone smoking a cheroot [cigar], one of the dozens he got through that extraordinary day,' reported *The Independent*, 'a moment of calm and silent consolation.' He returned to the Reuters screen after 10 minutes. Sterling remained 'flat as a pancake'.[19]

'It hasn't worked,' exclaimed a City trader over the trading room squawk-box. 'The only buyers of sterling are central banks.'[20] 'If anything, the pound went down,' commented a Bank official. 'We had always recognised that the markets might regard a rate rise as counter-productive.'[21] And thus it proved. 'The 2% rise was really a weapon of last resort,' a Treasury official told the *Sunday Times*. 'The effect was zilch. We were caught in a typhoon. We were blown off course by the sheer pressure and volume of resources pitted against us. We could not have done any more.' 'We knew that the game was over. Everything was out of control,'[22] said another.

The Bank's buying and the rate increase emboldened speculators to intensify their bets; the British authorities were rapidly using up their ammunition.

Short selling of sterling to the Bank of England was being conducted on a massive scale not only by traders but also by bank and corporate treasurers and asset managers who were becoming increasingly convinced that Britain would leave the ERM and devalue. Volumes were unprecedented. 'I can't stress enough the sheer scale of the selling,' said an awestruck adviser, 'It was as if an avalanche was coming at us.'[23]

Although the rate rise had no effect on the exchange rate, it had a dire impact on the stock market, sending the FTSE 100 index down 80 points, a 3.3% fall. The share price collapse generated a defiant 'ledge humour' on the part of some investors. 'You'll notice we've got our windows open today,' a UK fund manager observed to a visiting reporter from the *Financial Times*.[24] 'I knew the game was up,' recalled Lamont. 'I later told a journalist I felt like a TV surgeon in *Casualty* watching a heart monitor and realising that the patient was dead; all we needed to do now was to unplug the system. I wanted to suspend our membership of the ERM as quickly as possible and stop the haemorrhaging of our reserves. I asked Jeremy [Heywood] to arrange for me to see the PM at once, and to tell him that we were suspending our membership. I assumed that a meeting would happen immediately.'[25]

Heywood tried fruitlessly to telephone the prime minister. Major, determined to maintain a facade of normality, was in a long-scheduled meeting with Conservative backbenchers discussing their concerns.[26] Unable to make phone contact, Lamont and his entourage, comprising the governor, deputy governor, and officials Terry Burns and Sarah Hogg, went to Admiralty House to see him but had to wait on a sofa in a corridor. 'I could not fathom what could be more important than to make the decisions we had to make to announce our withdrawal from the ERM,' recollected Lamont.[27] Eventually Major appeared, 'joking with Tory MPs and looking extremely relaxed.' Major recalled the chancellor as 'white-faced' and 'downcast'.[28] The meeting got underway at 12.45pm. 'It hasn't worked,' said Lamont. 'They're still selling,' said Burns.[29]

The British authorities had been defeated by a combination of Schlesinger and the French referendum, said the chancellor. They had no alternative but a temporary suspension of ERM membership and they should do so immediately, giving other members 15 minutes' warning. It was the least bad option. Why suspension, not devaluation? Italy stood as a stark warning. Just two days earlier it had tried a 7% devaluation and the lira was already pinned to its new floor. Devaluing the pound would merely have given the markets another target to shoot at.[30] But, wondered Major, couldn't the Germans and French do more on the UK's behalf? He expressed concern about the damage British suspension might do the Maastricht treaty and questioned whether it would be possible for Britain to rejoin the ERM if it left.

Nothing had been resolved when just after 1pm the discussion was joined by Heseltine, Clarke and Hurd. 'I was astounded. I could not see why it was necessary to involve all these ministers,' commented Lamont. 'What could they contribute to discussions? There was an obvious danger that it would make it much harder to reach decisions, and in a financial crisis speed was of the essence… I outlined the situation once more making it quite clear that in my opinion we had no real option but to withdraw from the ERM there and then. The governor said that was also the clear view of the Bank of England.'[31]

Major outlined four options. One was to intervene further until the reserves were exhausted. The second, another interest rate rise of three percentage points to 15%. The third was a realignment of sterling in the ERM. Fourth, Britain could suspend ERM membership. He then went around the table for comment.[32] 'Hurd became agitated, insisting that everything was done according to the rules so as not to offend our partners,' recalled Lamont.[33] Hurd remembered being told 'every remedy had been tried and that we should immediately suspend British membership of the ERM… every minute of discussion cost the reserves £18m… I argued, and others agreed, that if this was to happen our partners should be told and the rules of the ERM followed. It could not be sensible to act in a way which would destroy trust in all our other decisions. Failure was one thing, panic another.'[34]

The discussion turned from suspension to the option of a further increase in the minimum lending rate. Heseltine and Clarke favoured another rate increase. 'They didn't really give any coherent reason for this except they wanted to stay in the ERM,' wrote Lamont, who said that in his view a rate increase would have no effect 'and certainly would not appear credible given the depressed state of the economy… and because it so obviously could not be maintained, it would not deter short selling.'[35] Major favoured a rate rise since 'we needed time to bring pressure on Germany and France to step up intervention on our behalf or to take helpful policy measures'.[36] Protesting that it would make no difference, Lamont agreed to a three percentage point rise to 15%. 'If that was the only way to demonstrate that we had no alternative but to suspend our membership, then I would do it,' he stated. 'It was agreed that if the rate increase did not work, we would then be prepared to consider suspending membership.'[37] 'The government wanted to keep open the possibility of returning to the EMS and so wanted to be seen as having tried everything,' explained an adviser. 'If 12% was all we had done, people would have said that we had held back from doing what was necessary. My great fear was that it would work.'[38]

Burns stated afterwards his surprise at how long it took to leave. 'In 1985, when the Treasury was looking at joining the ERM, [Treasury Second Permanent Secretary] Geoff Littler drew up a paper on the circumstances under which Britain could suspend intervention obligations at a time of extreme crisis. It was always anticipated that we would make use of this in an emergency.'[39] Clarke said afterwards: 'After the Bank of England put up interest rates by two percentage points and it didn't work, we should have left. But then Douglas Hurd put forward the opinion of the Foreign Office lawyers that we were under a treaty obligation to stay in the mechanism and carry on intervening… This was rather pedantic… Who was going to challenge us in the courts? The only person who could perhaps have claimed later that he was damaged would have been George Soros.'[40]

At 2.15pm, the Bank of England announced its intention to raise rates to 15%. 'Again, I watched the Reuters screen and, as before, the patient showed no signs of life,' recalled Lamont. 'This time I was relieved.'[41] He also looked at the television in the outer office, which was broadcasting public reactions to the announcement. One of those interviewed was a constituent who exclaimed: 'God's teeth. Another 3%. That's staggering… are you sure? It was only 2% before lunch.' A businessman said: 'I think it's April 1st.'[42]

It was the first time in living memory there had been two interest rate changes announced on the same day. The trading floor at a US bank in the City erupted with cheering, overheard by a visitor who observed that 'those buggers are making a lot of money out of all this.'[43] A trader commented, 'The pound's doing nothing. It's just sitting there.'[44] 'There's a bloke on the phone says he wants to buy sterling,' quipped a colleague, 'Says his name's Lamont.'[45] People laughed, and moved on to the next trade. 'The central banks were buying sterling and the rest of the world was selling,' recalled a trader, 'It was no contest.'[46] Paradoxically the second rate increase had a cheering effect on share prices, which surged upwards. The move was taken as a sign of weakness and the prelude to throwing in the ERM towel, meaning devaluation and rate cuts. The FTSE 100 closed eight points up on Wednesday.[47] 'When the rate rise to 12% was announced,' recalled Jim

Trott, who had a ringside seat in the Bank of England's dealing room, 'all the share screens went red. When the second rise to 15% was announced, they all went blue.'[48]

Major telephoned Pierre Bérégovoy and Helmut Kohl to inform them of the dire circumstances and request support. 'Bérégovoy was hugely supportive, and very agitated. The focus was partly on his own referendum. He was worried that the pressure would intensify.'[49] At a French Cabinet meeting that day, Bérégovoy could not resist a swipe against Major's predecessor: 'Britain is paying dearly for the policies of Mrs Thatcher.'[50]

Major tried to speak to Kohl but he rang back only after a relatively long time. Major told Kohl, 'If the pound left the ERM, the French franc could be next, and the system might soon collapse entirely.'[51] But Kohl replied that the affair was a matter for the Bundesbank: 'I am powerless to intervene.'[52]

Bérégovoy consulted German Finance Minister Theo Waigel and called Major back to tell him they had concluded the best way of stabilising the situation was for sterling to leave the ERM. Lamont received commiserations from fellow finance ministers, but no material help. Leigh-Pemberton reported back empty-handed, recounting that, astonishingly, Schlesinger had been 'unavailable' to speak to him.

At 4pm the Bank of England told other central banks sterling's ERM membership was being 'temporarily' suspended – four hours after the Treasury had intended, a delay that cost many billions of dollars from the reserves. In New York trading, sterling immediately fell 3% against the D-mark, reaping spectacular rewards for traders who had sold the currency (which they had themselves borrowed) at higher levels only 24 hours earlier.

Lamont and Major met at Admiralty House at 4.40pm. The chancellor reported the second rate rise had made no difference. Suspension of membership was the only option. They agreed to seek an emergency meeting of the European Monetary Committee to give formal agreement to the suspension. Nigel Wicks, the UK representative on the committee, was despatched to Brussels to convene the meeting. At 5pm Major and Lamont were joined by Hurd, Clarke and Heseltine, who 'reluctantly' agreed to sterling's suspension from the ERM. The Treasury insisted there should be no public comment on the suspension until the monetary committee had met. Lamont returned to the Treasury where he finalised the government statement and at 7.30pm stepped out to the courtyard to announce that the UK was bowing to the inevitable. 'An almost tangible sense of relief swept through the Treasury,' reported *The Independent*. 'Senior staff ordered pizzas and opened a couple of bottles of wine. They watched as, in New York, sterling immediately fell to DM 2.687.' Interviewed by *Independent Television News*, Mark Clarke, a currency trader in Bank of America's dealing room, told 8.5m viewers he had 'dumped' £500m of sterling and made £10m. Lamont, who was watching at the Treasury, shook his head and turned to the young official next to him. 'That's capitalism,' he said.[53] With sterling floating there was no point in maintaining the interest rate increase to 12%, so on Thursday morning the Bank of England announced its minimum lending rate had been cut to 10%, where it had been 22 hours earlier.

The European Monetary Committee met shortly before midnight in Brussels under Jean-Claude Trichet's chairmanship to formalise the ERM withdrawal. Wicks related how, 'within a few hours, Britain's foreign exchange reserves had been transformed from a plus of more than $20bn into a significant negative position.'[54] The committee first considered, and rejected, a British proposal for a general suspension of the ERM. Wicks then gave notification of Britain's unilateral temporary suspension of ERM participation. 'As always, Europe would be as difficult as possible,' recalled Lamont, 'but now it would make no difference what they decided. In the end the monetary committee decided shortly before midnight to agree to the suspension of sterling that I had announced at 7.30pm.'[55] Sterling was not the only ERM currency under pressure. Italy also suspended ERM participation in the meeting and Spain devalued the peseta by 5%.

Looking back on the day the universal sense among ministers and officials was an 'overwhelming emotion of disbelieving impotence'.[56] Leigh-Pemberton told friends he was overwhelmed by a terrible sense of failure. 'We were all pretty clear that it was an unmitigated disaster,' said a minister.[57] 'We left the business of government and economics on Wednesday morning and entered a casino,' a Treasury official told *The Observer*. 'No government is in absolute control over what is happening anymore. We are in the lap of the gods.'[58]

At the post-Black Wednesday Cabinet meeting, Lamont put a brave face on the disaster. According to a speaking note for Thursday 17 September that bears the hallmark of his adviser Jeremy Heywood, the chancellor affirmed,

'Yesterday's dramatic decision was determined solely by short-term market considerations, not by the state of the economy.'[59] Over the last four weeks, Lamont had been 'fighting an hour by hour battle to keep sterling within its bands without putting up interest rates.' He had tried 'every tactic in the book' – intervention, public statements and 'a massive loan programme designed to buttress the credibility of our ERM commitment'. Britain had put 'every conceivable pressure on the Germans at all levels to get them to relax monetary policy'. This included personal contacts with Helmut Kohl, Theo Waigel and Foreign Minister Klaus Kinkel in the German government as well as the Bank of England's dealings with the Bundesbank. Major and Lamont had 'persuaded' the Italians, French , Spanish and others 'to weigh in similarly with the Germans'.

The Bundesbank's 'modest cut' on Monday had been 'welcome' - but 'it came too late to halt an inexorable slide. Because all our efforts have been swimming continuously against a unique tidal wave' including 'repeated hints/rumours and so on emanating from the Bundesbank that they were looking for a devaluation of the pound… Things began to come to a head on Tuesday night when the president of the Bundesbank again allowed journalists to walk away with the impression that he favoured a realignment of the pound. The effect was devastating…' Interest rate increases were 'the final card' but 'even this proved futile. We faced a massive haemorrhage in our reserves, to the extent that threatened to exhaust our entire stock in one day.'

In a sign of senior officials enacting *Yes Minister*-type stratagems towards their political bosses, Andrew Turnbull, heading the Treasury's monetary department, and Terry Burns, the permanent secretary, took pains to shield the chancellor from too much bad news on the reserve losses.

In a detailed memo on whether and when sterling should rejoin the ERM – 'There can be no question of re-entering in a matter of weeks' – Turnbull wrote to Burns on 18 September: 'Our net reserves are negative. At the moment we can only intervene by undertaking more borrowing, much of which may have to be repaid in a few months. We need to replenish our usable reserves either by creaming off [intervening to prevent the pound from rising, involving buying foreign exchange] or a programme of longer-term borrowing.' After discussing the paper with Burns, Turnbull submitted his findings to the chancellor in the evening of 18 September with an identical message but one major amendment: the word 'negative' had been struck from the record. 'Our reserves,' Turnbull told Lamont in the adjusted message, were 'severely depleted'.[60]

Schlesinger's somewhat hapless attempts to calm nerves between the UK and Germany backfired when the German embassy in London sent to the *Financial Times* at the end of September a Bundesbank paper refuting suggestions that the Germans had given inadequate support to sterling – sparking a furious diplomatic row.[61]

Shortly afterwards, a month after Black Wednesday, Schlesinger met Queen Elizabeth on an official visit to Germany. She asked him 'whether speculators could really be so strong?' The Bundesbank president replied, 'Yes Madam, in a system of fixed exchange rates with high differentials in the rate of inflation, they can. They have a high chance, unfortunately.'[62]

Schlesinger vented his fatalistic view of the rumpus when he told the French ambassador to Bonn on 1 November that Britain's departure from the ERM had been 'inevitable'.[63] Alan Budd, the Treasury's chief economic adviser with a ringside seat at the spectacle, later summarised in 'slightly cruel' manner the 23-month adventure: 'We went into the ERM in despair and left in disgrace.'[64]

Aftermath

CHAPTER EIGHTEEN

Field of ruins

After Britain's September squalls, European currency unrest switched to the French franc. During four separate skirmishes in an 11-month period, the French and German monetary authorities engaged in frequently vitriolic confrontations, culminating in an uneasy truce in August 1993. Co-operation between the two countries was restored and France rescued its currency policy, which survived the entry into the euro in 1999 more or less intact – but at severe political and economic cost.

In the immediate aftermath of Black Wednesday, a wafer-thin French vote in favour of the Maastricht treaty in the 20 September referendum generated a storm of franc sales on foreign exchanges. On Tuesday 22 September Kohl visited Mitterrand in Paris to discuss the next stage of the Maastricht process. The French president, although enfeebled by prostate cancer, successfully cajoled the German chancellor to persuade the Bundesbank to take action to support the franc. Joachim Bitterlich, Kohl's foreign policy adviser, who accompanied the chancellor to Paris, reported:

> The president was not in the best of moods when he welcomed the chancellor and his small delegation. It was clear that something was troubling him deeply. A question from the chancellor elicited a short statement: 'The Bank of France has run out of funds, we have used up all the reserves against the speculators. We won't be able to avoid devaluing the franc and reinstating capital controls.' The chancellor composed himself – his understanding had been that the monetary front had quietened down – and asked the president if he could telephone Washington. The autumn meetings of the IMF and World Bank were taking place there, the finance minister and Bundesbank president were still there and he wanted to speak to them to hear their

assessment and get their views of the best way to proceed. Enough said: from the office of one of the president's colleagues we reached Messrs Schlesinger – not exactly a friend of the euro – Tietmeyer and Waigel. He [Kohl] discussed the situation with them and asked them to examine how best one could help the French. In contrast to a widely held opinion, Mitterrand on that day did not press the chancellor for a joint statement under which the Bundesbank would defend the franc in all circumstances. He was aware of the sensitivities on this subject on our side.[1]

According to detailed documents from the Elysée palace, the French president pressed Kohl on the issue much more fiercely than the German side has ever been willing to divulge. Both Schlesinger and Tietmeyer denied later that Kohl had given 'instructions' which would have contravened the Bundesbank Law; in his telephone conversations the chancellor had merely outlined 'points of view'. Underlining the sensitivity of the exchanges with Kohl, Waigel recorded in a personal memo on 22 September that – despite all contrary impressions – the Bundesbank's independence had been formally upheld as Kohl had left all final decisions to the central bank.

Mitterrand, however, was brutally frank. In his Paris conversation, he told Kohl France might have to leave the ERM 'unless other ways can be found to keep it alive'.[2] Mitterrand said 'billions [of dollars] of drugs money' were attacking the franc and blamed the Bundesbank for talking down other currencies following the cut in German interest rates the previous week. 'The speculation has been unleashed. It will be enough if we hold out for three days, and then it will have failed. I am aware of the independence of the Bundesbank, but what does it want? To remain the last one standing on a field of ruins? Because it will be a field of ruins.'

Showing characteristic insouciance on monetary issues, Kohl claimed he was unaware of the gravity of the crisis. 'I'm surprised by your dramatic tone. People told me yesterday that everything was calming down. I read Bérégovoy's letter in the aeroplane. I don't understand.'

Kohl used a break in his talks in Paris to initiate a remarkable series of trans-Atlantic telephone exchanges, starting with Horst Köhler, Waigel's deputy in the German finance ministry. After the first call, Kohl returned to the meeting with Mitterrand. According to the Elysée palace transcript, Kohl declared that whatever action to be taken would have to remain secret.

Kohl: 'They have told me that the situation is not that serious and the Bundesbank is prepared to help. It will announce that it will not raise rates, is considering a rate cut and will extend a further $5bn credit line to defend the franc.'

Mitterrand: 'Only implacable political will can stop the speculation. We have to show that.'

Kohl: 'I cannot say that the parity will be maintained. I cannot go over the head of the Bundesbank. That's not my business. That is the Bundesbank's business. This should not appear like political manipulation. I had a terrible discussion with the Bundesbank last week. That has become known. I cannot start that again. I will try, all the same, to see if we can obtain a rapid declaration from the governors. But I don't wish anyone to know about this. If I am asked, on coming out of here, I will say that we have discussed the situation in Europe after the referendum. As to monetary affairs, I will say that the discussions have taken place in Washington.'[3]

At a simultaneous meeting in Washington during the annual gatherings of the IMF and World Bank, Jean-Claude Trichet as director of the French Treasury was fighting a rearguard action to preserve the franc's ERM parity against fierce opposition from Helmut Schlesinger. The Bundesbank president was at the helm of a strong German delegation that included his colleagues Tietmeyer and Issing, Finance Minister Theo Waigel, and Horst Köhler, state secretary at the finance ministry.[4] Jacques de Larosière, governor of the Banque de France, and Michel Sapin, finance minister, had already left Washington to prepare for a Concorde flight back to Paris, ready for the eventuality of a franc devaluation. Pressure on the franc was the subject of a remarkable series of trans-Atlantic telephone exchanges.

After holding an initial conversation with Köhler while he was in the Elysée palace, Kohl retired with his delegation to a Parisian restaurant where he spoke again with Tietmeyer and Schlesinger in Washington, prodding the Germans into a flurry of activity. Trichet wanted a declaration that the franc's parity was inviolable. Schlesinger initially refused to sign, saying France must devalue: 'France has done nothing to defend the franc! Nothing serious! It has not even made use of our offer to buy francs in Frankfurt for your account.' Trichet declared himself 'stupefied and indignant', affirming that Schlesinger was speaking 'the language of breakdown'. Trichet gave a long exposition of why a franc devaluation was unjustified, declaring to Köhler during a break in the meeting how Germany was making a mistake 'if they thought they could treat us in the same way that England and Italy had been treated quantitatively and qualitatively. We were not comparable, neither economically, nor politically, nor strategically.'[5]

After the phone calls with Kohl, the German side showed conciliation. Köhler said the Germans would accept a common declaration. Schlesinger said he would sign it only if the two other directorate members at the meeting, Tietmeyer and Issing, agreed. The Bundesbank said it would raise total credits to the Banque de France to DM39bn – DM4bn more than granted to the Bank of England during the previous week's turmoil.[6] Citing the principles of the 1978 Emminger letter, Schlesinger declared that Bundesbank support could not be unlimited. If automatic intervention to support the franc at its ERM floor exceeded DM10bn, Germany would convene the European Monetary Committee as a prelude to a franc devaluation.

After all-night preparations in Paris, the French and German central banks and finance ministries published a joint statement early on 23 September 1992, declaring the sanctity of the D-mark-franc parity. Accompanied by large-scale central bank intervention funded by the Bundesbank (totalling $32bn in the week to 23 September), increases in money market interest rates in France and cuts in Germany, the announcement succeeded temporarily in quelling anti-franc speculation. 'Germany had its own interest in signing this statement,' Sapin said, because Schlesinger saw the threat to Germany's economic position as a result of the monetary consequences of unification. 'Preventing a large franc devaluation against the D-mark was important to help not just the French but also the German economy.'[7] Mitterrand's economic advisers told him how France's hard line had paid off: 'Schlesinger gave in only when the French delegation broke off the negotiations and when it was clear that we would not devalue but would require the Germans to respect or repudiate its EMS obligations.'[8]

France was aware of Britain's sensitivities about Germany's more generous treatment of the French than of the UK. French officials agreed to keep secret the nature of Kohl's conversation with Mitterrand on 22 September. According to an internal Elysée palace note, 'We have been instructed to say nothing to the press, so as not to put Kohl in difficulty, and not to give credibility to the idea that a political authority could give instructions to central banks.'[9] When John Major visited Mitterrand in Paris a week later, the two leaders swapped criticism of the Bundesbank. Major told Mitterrand, 'We believe in London that the Bundesbank gave all the information necessary [to the foreign exchange markets] to damage sterling... The shock was caused by Schlesinger's remarks... We could no longer save the pound. The Bundesbank refused to lower its rates any more. We increased ours by 2% and then by 5%, without effect. We had no choice but to leave the system.' Mitterrand responded laconically that Schlesinger had shown 'a certain brutality'.[10]

The hard-won Franco-German compromises by no means marked the end of currency hostilities. November brought devaluations of the Spanish peseta and Portuguese escudo. The Banque de France again had to intervene to prevent the franc from falling to its ERM floor. Trichet recorded in December, 'The situation is extremely dangerous. The Anglo-Saxon markets, in London and New York, are playing for the destruction of the European Monetary System.'[11] Prime Minister Bérégovoy wrote to Kohl urging the Bundesbank to cut rates. 'A slowdown in economic activity in Europe has deep repercussions on employment, both in France and in Germany... I must alert you once more to the consequences.' The plea was ignored – the Bundesbank delayed further cuts in its leading interest rates until February 1993.

Further unrest hit another weaker currency in the ERM, the Irish pound, which was devalued in February amid an upsurge in attacks on the franc. Heavy defeat for Bérégovoy's Socialist government in the March 1993 parliamentary elections lifted confidence in the French economy. Depressed by the election result and rumours that he had been involved in a corruption scandal, Bérégovoy – one of the principal architects of the 'hard franc' policy – shot himself on 1 May.

Mitterrand's new prime minister was Edouard Balladur. The former finance minister conspicuously strengthened his previously lukewarm support for monetary union and – benefiting from close links to both de Larosière and Trichet (who succeeded de Larosière as Banque de France governor in January 1994) – started the process of making the French central bank independent. France accelerated interest rate cuts. For a time, from mid-June onwards, short-term French interest rates fell below

German levels. In an unguarded radio interview on 24 June 1993, Edmond Alphandéry, Balladur's new finance minister, suggested that a forthcoming Franco-German economic meeting scheduled for July should agree a further cut in German rates. The Germans interpreted the statement as undermining the Bundesbank's independence and cancelled the meeting.

When the Bundesbank did cut its discount and Lombard rates on 1 July, the D-mark ominously strengthened. Banque de France intervention to support the franc rose steadily. Balladur asked Jacques Delors, the European Commission president, to phone Kohl to seek a resolution. A secret nocturnal Franco-German meeting in Munich on 22 July failed to calm the storm. The French asked for renewed Bundesbank 'swap' credits of DM15bn, which the Germans agreed on condition France raised interest rates. The Bundesbank agreed to discuss a small Lombard rate cut, calming the foreign exchanges until Reimut Jochimsen, a querulous Bundesbank council member and the bane of Britain during the September 1992 crisis, ruled out rate cuts during a lunchtime TV interview – sparking extra French intervention to shore up the franc.

Franco-German currency antagonism reached a peak after the Bundesbank – despite a larger-than-promised 0.5 percentage point cut in its Lombard rate – kept its discount rate unchanged on 29 July. Kohl and Balladur agreed the French and German monetary authorities would meet again in Paris the next day, 30 July. Balladur wrote to Kohl protesting that the Bundesbank's Lombard rate cut was 'insufficient', proclaiming the latest crisis had cost France $27bn in intervention.[12] Balladur suggested unlimited Bundesbank intervention, an 'immediate and adequate' cut in interest rates, and direct purchases of francs for the Bundesbank's own reserves. Balladur accompanied the proposal – highly reminiscent of various British pleas for Bundesbank help in the 1970s and 1980s – by dispatching letters to other European governments suggesting Germany should quit the ERM to lower tensions for the other currencies, a move that would have given France the long prized 'anchor role' in Europe.

At 10.30am on Friday 30 July 1993, amid heavy international franc selling – the Banque de France was intervening with purchases of $100m of francs per minute at one stage – Waigel, Schlesinger, Tietmeyer and Gert Haller, the new finance ministry state secretary, arrived irritated and late at the Paris finance ministry's new headquarters in eastern Paris. The

German visitors' arrival was delayed because the French authorities sent slow-moving mini-buses, not the normal sleek limousines, to meet them at the military airport southwest of the city. Waigel told Alphandéry that Balladur's suggestions were 'unacceptable'. Schlesinger commented later: 'The French received us very coldly. We felt that it was like standing in the Hall of Mirrors of Versailles, ready to sign the German capitulation. It was made clear that either we had to carry out unlimited intervention in favour of the franc, or that Germany had to leave the EMS.' De Larosière declared the French authorities were letting the franc fall to its ERM floor – triggering unlimited automatic support intervention under the EMS.

The French were running out of reserves, just as the British had done nine months earlier. As the meeting was about to end, Schlesinger cold-bloodedly pointed out the enormous sums the French had borrowed to defend the franc. The Banque de France owed the Bundesbank DM34bn, and Germany would soon request repayment.

The German foursome flew to Austria on the afternoon of 30 July to see Kohl in his holiday residence. The chancellor backed the Bundesbank's uncompromising line and Waigel's stated desire to free the Bundesbank from obligatory intervention on Monday morning. This time, unlike the pre-Black Wednesday weekend when France failed to organise a realignment meeting, Germany unilaterally convened the European Monetary Committee for Saturday 31 July, followed by a session with finance ministers and central bank governors on Sunday. After many hours of vexatious disagreement, the crisis was resolved at around 2am on Monday 2 August – just before currency trading re-opened in the Far East – through a drastic widening of the ERM's fluctuation band to 15% either side of a central rate, making an overall margin of 30%.[13]

The French proposal for the Germans to leave the EMS was rejected after the Dutch said they would follow the D-mark out of the system, a move propounded by the Belgians too. De Larosière said Balladur's initial proposal of a 6% fluctuation band would be insufficient to deter speculators: 'It would be like putting a big piece of raw meat in front of lions. It would be swallowed in two to three days.'[14] Britain's pro-European Chancellor Kenneth Clarke, who had replaced Lamont in June, attended the Brussels meeting. Just as the meeting appeared to be breaking up without agreement, Clarke intervened forcibly late at night to promote the growing consensus on wider bands.[15]

Allowing currencies to fluctuate by an exceptionally wide margin effectively suspended the ERM – but the emergency measure avoided formal devaluations and prevented speculators from making profits. As Balladur said: 'We fought the speculators and we won.'[16]

At the weekly French Cabinet meeting two days afterwards, Mitterrand acknowledged the optimal solution would have been to persuade the Germans to leave the ERM. 'The difficulties stem from Germany's problems in managing its reunification and trying to make the other Europeans pay for it.'[17]

Looking back at the lessons of the 1990s, Christian Noyer, chief of staff at the finance ministry during the tumult, who later became director of the Treasury and governor of the Banque de France, said France, Germany and the UK missed an opportunity after German unification to let the D-mark find its own level through floating. The three countries didn't think of this because they were 'fragmented'.[18] Noyer said monetary scrimmages with the Germans hardened French determination to press on with monetary union – to ensure past sacrifices had not been in vain. 'If France had followed the path of floating, we would have devalued by perhaps around 20% at the same time as Italy and Britain. By not doing that, France saved EMU.'

CHAPTER NINETEEN

Lightning conductor

Norman Lamont was not alone in observing that, if he had resigned the chancellorship immediately after Black Wednesday, John Major's position would have been vulnerable. Major, not Lamont, had been the decisive influence in persuading Thatcher to sign up in 1990 to the ERM. Lamont, in lightning conductor mode, bore an unconscionable share of the political fallout. In the weeks leading up to September 1992 he was at the centre of sporadic discussions in Whitehall over the sustainability of the government's ERM policy. But, like other chancellors before him, Lamont found himself boxed in on all sides. Some officials had become convinced, when sterling came under pressure in July, that the government would have to raise interest rates if it was serious about retaining the pound's position. However a rise in interest rates at that stage would have been politically unacceptable, and economically inappropriate.

Black Wednesday led to some attempted revisions of history. Some ministers and others maintained the economic recovery was not 'subsequent' and had begun in spring 1992. But no one at the time thought economic recovery had begun before Black Wednesday, just as no one believed the economy could withstand a rise in interest rates. The 'bridging policy' devised by the Treasury and the Bank of England – aimed, with the help of a large foreign credit, at overcoming a series of chasms leading up to the 20 September French referendum – ended in failure.

In this ignominious context, it is hardly surprising that some of Lamont's September remarks were later taken out of context. In the week after sterling left the ERM, he was asked at a press conference during the annual IMF-World Bank meetings in Washington why he was looking so cheerful. 'Well,' Lamont replied, 'it is a very beautiful morning, but it is funny you should say that. My wife said she heard me singing in the bath this morning.'[1]

Lamont had certainly not sung in Bath, where he chaired the acrimonious finance ministers meeting on 5 September and angered Helmut Schlesinger, the Bundesbank president, by persistently demanding a German interest rate cut. Years later Lamont – who always (accurately) maintained he was acting on behalf of other ERM members affected by high German rates, not just the UK – said, 'That was a last resort. I knew what the constitutional position of the Bundesbank was and that they were not likely to yield to our demands.'[2] In Schlesinger's position, he added, 'I might have behaved in a similar way.'[3]

After his string of upsets, Lamont lasted at the Treasury until May 1993, when he was effectively sacked and replaced by Kenneth Clarke, the previous home secretary. Lamont's removal had less to do with his post-Black Wednesday record as chancellor than with his capacity for embroiling himself in colourful extra-parliamentary episodes, which made him a target for the tabloids. Lamont's professional performance during the closing months of his chancellorship deserves – but has not always received – due praise. He was responsible for a series of innovations that turned out to be both benign and relatively long-lasting.

Lamont set in place a new monetary policy which was crowned in 1997 under his successor-but-one Gordon Brown with the operational independence of the Bank of England and the establishment of the rate-setting Monetary Policy Committee. One of the most convincing changes was the introduction in October 1992 of the latest, and hitherto most successful, in a series of British economic policy panaceas – the inflation target.[4] Regular monthly meetings between the chancellor and the governor of the Bank of England were instituted at the same time as the quarterly inflation report as a new tool for economic guidance.

All this came against the background of financial market unrest and political uncertainty. Something had to be done to bring about calm, and the glimmerings of operational independence for the Bank of England appeared the right remedy. While in office Lamont had flirted with the idea of Bank independence. But, just as Thatcher had rebuffed Nigel Lawson in this matter, so too did Major object to putting interest rate decisions in the hands of unelected officials.

In his resignation statement in the House of Commons, Lamont recognised how, in choosing to stay on as chancellor after Black Wednesday, he had partly acted as a shield for the prime minister. '[Major] emphasised that he regarded the attacks on me as coded attacks on himself, so I decided that my duty and loyalty was to the prime minister and that I should remain in office.'[5] Lamont's bitterness showed through: 'Since the war only two Conservative chancellors have been responsible for bringing inflation down to below 2%. Both of them were sacked.' Memorably, he declared that Major gave the impression of being 'in office but not in power' and was over-prone to 'short-termism… Unless this approach is changed, the government will not survive.'

Ken Clarke was entering the Treasury at a propitious time. 'Much of the hard work has been done and he should be able to enjoy increasingly encouraging trends for a long time to come.' He affirmed that 'nothing would be more effective in establishing the government's credibility than… to make the Bank of England independent… Now that we are outside the ERM, the need is even more urgent. Britain is one of the few countries where monetary policy remains firmly in political hands, and the pressures on politicians to take policy decisions for political reasons can be quite irresistible.' Lamont blamed the breakdown of the ERM policy on 'German policy [which] developed in a way which, in my view, was mistaken and which was not anticipated.' Lamont spelled out some potent political reasons why he did not resign immediately, contrasting his position with that of two former Labour chancellors, Sir Stafford Cripps, who did not resign after devaluing the pound in 1949, and James Callaghan, at the Treasury in 1967, who did.

> Membership of the exchange rate mechanism was the policy of the whole government; and as the prime minister said, I was implementing government policy. Our entry was not a decision in which I myself played any part. It was, however, a decision made after a whole decade of fierce public and private argument… When the prime minister reappointed me after the [1992] general election, I told him two things: first, that I did not wish to remain chancellor for very long; and, secondly, that he did not owe me any debt or any obligation. On 16 September, he made it clear to me in writing that he had no intention of resigning himself, and that I should not do so either.

John Smith, the Labour party's shadow chancellor, said in somewhat back-handed fashion that Lamont's statement was 'as effective a speech as any he made when he was in office'.[6] Debates over the future role of the central bank and the responsibility for the September breakdown formed the background to a dramatic economic recovery in 1992-97. The contrast with the period immediately before Black Wednesday – and with other European economies – was extraordinary. British GDP contracted by 1.1% in 1990, and grew only anaemically by 0.7% and 0.4% in 1991 and 1992 respectively, while German GDP grew 5.7% in 1990, 5% in 1991 and 1.5% in 1992.

The longer-term aftermath can be divided into three periods, delineated by the 1999 birth of the euro and the 2008-09 crisis. In each of the three periods, UK output outperformed that of the two major continental economies, while unemployment was also lower. In the periods 1992-99, 1999-2009 and 2009-16, UK GDP rose by an annual average of 2.7%, 2.5% and 1.2% respectively, compared with 1.4%, 1.6% and 1.0% in Germany and 2.0%, 1.9% and 0.6% in France. Unemployment in 1992-99, 1999-2009 and 2009-16 was 8.2%, 5.2% and 7.0% in the UK, 8.4%, 9.0% and 5.6% in Germany, and 10.5%, 8.5% and 9.8% in France. Inflation was comparable in all three periods.

Progressive reductions in interest rates afforded by release from the constraints of the ERM strengthened the conditions for low inflationary growth. A further benefit stemmed from the competitive boost of a weaker pound as the sterling-D-mark rate fell in the two years after September 1992 to below DM2.2 from its central rate of DM2.95. Conventional wisdom held that a devaluation of such proportions would be inflationary, but it was not. Clarke inherited a much more benign economic picture. He observed, 'I gained the sense that inflationary pressure in the real economy was weakening all the time. I did not believe that the devaluation would lead to wage inflation.' He argued with Treasury officials 'that globalisation and the supply-side reforms must have done something to change the conditions of the 1980s. People in China were going to keep inflation down.' Major spotted what had changed. In the Lamont-Clarke periods under his prime ministerial tutelage, wage earnings – the main element of past inflationary surges of the past – never rose by more than half the lowest rate of increase in the 1980s.

Clarke recognised early on what has since become a commonplace. His insight accords well with the theory that chancellors – Clarke studied law at Cambridge – don't necessarily have to be economists. The Clarke chancellorship has taken on the allure of something close to a golden era, certainly in comparison to UK and international experience since the 2008 financial crisis. For this feat, Major knew he would reap no thanks.

In the same way as Labour in the 1970s could not and did not recover from the 1976 IMF crisis, the Major government would gain no forgiveness for Black Wednesday or the well-publicised damage to the reserves wreaked by George Soros and others. To make matters worse, Major had to deal with a band of Conservative Eurosceptics impelled by Thatcher, harrying him at every step of the journey to win ratification of the Maastricht treaty.

There can be little doubt that, had Britain not faced the constraints of the ERM, economic policy in 1992 could have been relaxed sooner. But there is a beguiling rationalisation, shared not only by Lamont but also by Alan Budd, the Treasury's chief economic adviser at the time, that membership of the ERM had enabled the government to remove inflation from the system, whereas a more gradualist approach would have run up against political hurdles. 'Membership of the ERM was not a very worthy episode,' Budd said in his Wincott lecture in 2004. 'Nevertheless, we are still enjoying the benefits of it.'

Membership of the ERM forced the UK to maintain the policies that brought inflation down to the levels at which it has stayed ever since. Norman Lamont, in the role of Ulysses, was tied to the mast, his ears stuffed with wax, so that he was unable to hear the siren calls for reflation... While we remained a member we were forced to adopt a policy that prolonged a recession. Those extra two years brought inflation down to levels that we have been able to maintain ever since. I do not believe that, in the circumstances of the time, the same effect could have been achieved by other means. The policies that were put in place after we left, starting with the system introduced in October 1992 and culminating in the establishment of the Monetary Policy Committee in 1997, allowed the benefits of ERM membership to be sustained.[7]

Budd pointed out, too, the extraordinary resilience of the exchange rate as the pound strengthened after the establishment of the euro in 1999 and the relative weakening of the German currency within the new single monetary framework. Budd's analysis lends credence to the overall Treasury view, backed by Terry Burns and others, that the basic problem with Britain's ERM policy in 1990-92 was the level not of the exchange rate, but of interest rates. Translating sterling's €1.50 rate in the early years of the 21st century into the equivalent D-mark level, Budd declared, 'Although departure from the ERM was followed by a significant depreciation as sterling appeared to settle at around DM2.25-2.50, since 1997 the rate seems to have settled, with remarkable stability, around DM2.95: the original central ERM rate.' The Budd view tends to gloss over the cost in terms of extra unemployment, bankruptcies and house repossessions of the extra disinflationary impact of maintaining ERM membership to the bitter end. Yet it is important, too, to stress ERM membership may have aggravated the recession, but did not cause it. As Keynesian economist Christopher Dow observed, the recession was the result of 'the rebound from the previous boom psychology. Collective, manic euphoria which pushed up prices and encouraged many to go into debt left the economy exhausted.'[8]

The ERM fiasco undoubtedly affected British attitudes towards the euro. Labour unexpectedly benefited from Major's diplomatic coup in negotiating Britain's 'opt out' from the single currency at Maastricht. Even critics who are fierce opponents of Gordon Brown tend to give him credit for keeping the country out of the euro, but it was Major who paved the way. During 1993-97, Clarke became the third chancellor in succession to advocate independence for the Bank of England and be overruled by a prime minister. But he prepared the way by making the Bank more transparent. In spring 1994 he began publishing the minutes of the monthly meetings of chancellor and governor which, following Eddie George's replacement of Leigh-Pemberton at the helm of the Bank in 1993, became known as 'the Ken and Eddie Show'. Clarke also put an end to Treasury censorship of the Bank's quarterly bulletin and inflation report, as well as Bank speeches.

One of the advantages of the period of sustained growth during the Clarke chancellorship was that the fiscal position improved. Clarke was proud of his reputation for fiscal caution and was criticised by colleagues for not going in for an electioneering 'give-away' budget in 1997. As far as Clarke was concerned, it would have been pointless. He thought he had restored the Conservatives' reputation for economic competence, but this would not help in the election: 'It was obvious that we were going to be massacred.'[9] That was what happened in the May 1997 election which ushered in Tony Blair and Gordon Brown as two successive Labour prime ministers until 2010, preaching an economic policy of 'prudence with a purpose' – just one of Black Wednesday's long-lived legacies.

CHAPTER TWENTY

Shock and survival

One of the longer-run consequences of the September 1992 crisis and its turbulent Franco-German aftermath was to weaken the Bundesbank's resistance to Europe's monetary unification. Whereas Schlesinger was unremittingly stringent about the prospects for monetary union during his time as Pöhl's vice president and his turbulent period as president between 1991-93, he became noticeably milder at the end of his mandate. In retirement, Schlesinger gave signals of support for the project – partly on the grounds that he saw it as his patriotic duty to support Chancellor Helmut Kohl.[1]

Otmar Issing, the Bundesbank's director in charge of economic affairs between 1990-98, who later took on the same job at the European Central Bank, was another hawk who changed his tune. He summed up the overall reasons for the blunting of the Bundesbank's habitual defiance: 'The decisive moment came with the currency crises of 1992-93. The status quo was not tenable. We faced a 30% devaluation of the lira. Some companies in southern Germany competing with Italy went bankrupt. There was a danger of controls on movement of goods. I and others concluded that the common market would not survive another crisis of this dimension.'[2]

Hans Tietmeyer, the long-time Bonn state secretary who moved to Frankfurt in 1990 and became Schlesinger's deputy and then president in 1993, was a member of Kohl's Christian Democratic Union. A man whose bluntness earned him the moniker of 'the Bundesbank's blunderbuss', Tietmeyer doggedly kept up a barrage of demands that Germany's monetary partners would face great strains in earning the right to take over the D-mark's mantle. 'A country with insufficient convergence could quickly reach the limits of its adaptability.'[3]

Yet behind Tietmeyer's harsh rhetoric was an underlying political complicity with Kohl. Once he took the top seat, Tietmeyer saw it as part of his duty to prepare the way for economic and monetary union. Germany's insistence on the other countries maintaining maximum monetary probity was undermined by Germany's own difficulties in meeting the Maastricht economic convergence criteria. As a result of the post-Black Wednesday economic slowdown the Germans faced hurdles in meeting the most sensitive of the chosen yardsticks – restricting public sector deficits to 3% of GDP. One key condition for progress towards EMU was relatively buoyant growth, as a means of returning public finances to some semblance of order. Given his carefully honed hawkish character, Tietmeyer played a strong role in helping achieve that condition. But, in view of this reputation, he did not take kindly to being reminded that he is the only Bundesbank president who did not once raise the bank's key interest rates.

The shock of the 1992-93 upsets, combined with the weakening of Germany's own capacity for imposing stringent conditions, provides a strong reason for Europe's collective failure in the 1990s to prevent serious design flaws becoming ingrained in the fabric of monetary union. The shortcomings were obscured for a while by the euro's relatively problem-free technical introduction, the enlargement of the euro area to include additional countries (led by Greece in 2001), and the initially successful adaptation to the trans-Atlantic financial crisis.

However, when intractable difficulties started to break out with the realisation of the full extent of the Greek debt malaise in 2010, it became clear how dependent the euro had become on a range of support and intervention measures, assembled through laborious compromises of ever greater complexity. The battery of rescue procedures, described with inscrutable technical acronyms, represents a significant reversal from the euro's original ideals of a self-regulating economy.

Instead, Europe found itself saddled with a new set of rules and procedures that achieved the prime goal of preventing the euro from collapsing, yet made the overall edifice of the single currency further removed from ordinary European citizens. Permanently fixed exchange rates and stable interest rates appeared to give greater security, but the absence of financial market fluctuations snuffed out the possibility for adverse capital flows to impose corrective pressure on errant governments to change policies. Against this background, the technocrats at the heart of the euro area developed a dangerous complacency.

The prime purveyor of unbridled optimism was the European Commission. In May 2008, just before the ECB's 10th anniversary, the Commission published a 328-page brochure gushing with exaggerated praise. Just two pages pointed to the problem of growing internal imbalances.[4] On its website, the Commission published a series of reassuring 'facts' about monetary union and denounced as 'myth' the assertion that 'some euro area member states suffer from economic problems in others'.[5] The truth was far more positive, the Commission affirmed: 'Governments coordinate their economic policies to ensure that all economies work harmoniously together... The single currency itself also acts as a protective shield against external shocks... Existing coordinating mechanisms mean that decisions can be taken quickly and smoothly – both in economic good times, and in the event of economic and financial difficulties.' Herman Van Rompuy, the scholarly former Belgian prime minister who, in 2010, became president of the European Council, the EU's governing body, admitted the euro's relatively problem-free start 'was like some kind of sleeping pill, some kind of drug'.[6] No less a person than Jacques Delors, former French finance minister and president of the Commission during the formative pre-single currency years of the 1980s, took aim in 2012 at Europe's collective errors.

> If the finance ministers had wanted to get a clearer picture of the situation, they could have seen Ireland's extravagant behaviour with its banks, Spain's equally extravagant behaviour with mortgage lending, Greece's dissimulation of its real statistics. But they turned a blind eye. That is why I have always considered, since the beginning of the crisis, that the Eurogroup was morally and politically responsible for the crisis and that it should have reacted as early as 2008 to rectify its mistakes... Spain, Greece, Ireland, Portugal and others thought they could make mistakes, protected by the euro. The trade balance between countries was disregarded. Nobody was concerned about that... At what moment did the governor of the [Central] Bank of Ireland, the governor of the Bank of Spain or other governors tell the ECB governing council that something was wrong? They did not say anything, nobody said a word. Therefore, they too are responsible for this situation. So, this is no time for them to lecture others.[7]

Another broadside was launched by Mario Draghi, the Italian technocrat and banker who took over from Jean-Claude Trichet as ECB president in November 2011. In 2013 Draghi accused 'all the actors' in monetary union of suffering from 'long, complacent amnesia'. They had ignored for years the risks that were building up. Draghi had been director of the Italian Treasury between 1991-2001. He then worked for US investment bank Goldman Sachs before becoming governor of the Banca d'Italia between 2005-11. He accurately portrayed the division of Europe, separating 'countries with positive trade balances and sound budgets from those with growing budget deficits and external deficits... No one ever imagined that the monetary union could become a union divided between permanent creditors and permanent debtors, where the former would perpetually lend money and credibility to the latter.' In fact, as Draghi and others later realised, countries that transgressed against economic laws by living beyond their means were building up invisible penalties that they – and others – would discharge only later. The trail of unpaid debts and festering grievances would extend far into the future.

Five mutually reinforcing miscalculations contributed to the slow-burn build-up. First, the ECB's one-sided focus on achieving its 2% inflation target diverted attention from problems in other fields, such as the stability of banks in the euro area. The ECB cannot be blamed for undue concentration on combating price rises, for its stance reflected political realities in Europe, particularly Germany's insistence that the new monetary system had to be built on Bundesbank-style anti-inflation rigour. However, excessive emphasis on fighting inflation – at a time when realising this goal was made significantly easier by globalisation-induced downward world-wide pressure on manufactured goods prices – encouraged complacency and hampered analysis of other policy areas where failures were looming. The ability to commit home-made mistakes was not a field, however, where the Europeans had a monopoly. Pre-financial crisis blunders by monetary authorities in the US and Britain were equally egregious.

Second, the belief that the 'one size fits all' monetary policy would lead to a symmetrical distribution of pain and gain was illusory. It was expected that faster-growing countries with above-average inflation and low interest rates at the beginning of monetary union would gain transitory benefits, but would suffer negative effects later, through reduced competitiveness that could no longer be rectified by devaluation. At the same time, low-inflation, low-growth countries such as Germany, which were held back at the beginning of the 2000s by interest rates that were too high for their own economic situation, would recover later, and this would help the rest of Europe. But these trends were not self-compensating. Germany used the earlier years of subdued growth to strengthen fundamentally its economic structures and has since been reaping the gains. Other countries enjoyed low interest rates and short-lived expansion without addressing structural reforms, and have subsequently paid the price. Overall, the costs exceeded the rewards, and over the lifetime of the euro the single currency has brought Europe a net deflationary bias.

The third error relates to the distortions in competitiveness that inevitably occur in a fixed exchange rate system that unites countries with different developments in prices and productivity. The idea was that these distortions could be reversed relatively easily, using a self-regulating process. Unfortunately, this has proved not to be the case. The early years of the euro opened a competitiveness gap of around 30% between Germany and southern European countries. This then started to close as the credit crisis and associated banking weaknesses ended the ability of peripheral countries to borrow their way out of trouble. The competitiveness distortions are being reversed less rapidly than required because Germany (like other creditor countries, such as the Netherlands) appears to be unwilling to undergo a period of radical reflation and weakening competitiveness to balance the debtor states' weakness. Those looking for economic stimulus and significantly higher inflation in Germany to rescue Europe's stragglers will be disappointed.

Fourth, Europe had to retreat from the misplaced belief that low-cost financing could be arranged in perpetuity for countries with extreme current account surpluses and deficits. Politicians and technocrats knew the euro would be immune to currency crises. But they overlooked the fact that the system could be prone to credit crises, as lenders demanded higher interest rates on debt that was perceived to be of increasingly higher risk, even (or especially) after years of apparent convergence on the bond markets. The refusal of private sector creditors to provide more cash for the indigent peripheral states brought in official lenders and harsh adjustment programmes that forcibly reduced the peripheral states' payments deficits, but allowed the creditor states to carry on generating surpluses. The burden of adjustment has been excessively skewed towards the deficit countries.

Fifth, finance ministers and central banks geared policies to limiting public debt and budget deficits while neglecting growth in private sector debt, which proved to be the euro bloc's point of weakness. Through the so-called Stability and Growth Pact agreed in 1997, euro members brought in rules for public debt monitoring. These were subsequently overridden by Germany and France during their phases of economic weakness in 2003-05, then suspended during the financial crisis, only to be reintroduced afterwards in modified form. However, by itself public debt provided an insufficient guide to the dangerous imbalances opening up: Ireland and Spain both registered budgetary surpluses in the years before their respective economic crashes. The formal rules of monetary union prevented policy-makers from looking at the explosive accumulation of private sector debt, with disastrous consequences. The arrival of an overtly pro-European French president in the form of Emmanuel Macron may provide a chance for France and Germany to break the deadlock. But, on analysis of history over the past 40 years, it would be foolish to pretend that the chances of success are high.

CHAPTER TWENTY ONE

First and second Brexit

There is doubt whether 16 September 1992 represented 'the first Brexit'. Some might date the first schism with Europe to Henry VIII's 1530s break with the Church of Rome or to the departure of Roman legions from England around 400AD. There may be parallels between the ERM withdrawal and the retreat of the British Expeditionary Force from Dunkirk in 1940, which, as Churchill said, was no victory – 'wars are not won by evacuations'[1] – but, like the European setback in 1992, allowed Britain to regroup its forces and regain ground and even glory in the years thereafter. Through whatever lens it is viewed, the chronicle of Britain's entanglement with the ERM undoubtedly represents a major landmark in the UK's European history.

Having advanced separately alongside the creation of EEC institutions and the march of economic integration in the 1950s and 1960s, Britain, by entering the European Community in 1973, established significant convergence with the continent. However, Britain's participation in Europe's monetary arrangement, the snake, lasted but a few weeks and sterling and the British economy developed on a semi-detached path through the rest of the 1970s and during the ERM's formative 1980s. Joining the ERM in October 1990 marked a major departure; Britain, it seemed, had become a full European participant. Then came the disputes over the Maastricht treaty, Black Wednesday and Britain's traumatic exit from the ERM – a reversion to the UK's traditional distance from the European core. The experience of 16 September contributed to the discredit and later electoral defeat of John Major's administration and to Chancellor Gordon Brown's reluctance to join the euro after Labour took power in 1997. A logical next step was the referendum rejection of EU membership and a return to the separation of the 1950s and 1960s. Thus, for Britain, the ERM crisis constituted a critical inflection point that can be regarded as 'the first Brexit'.

A major impulse for western European integration was the unsettled state of Germany, suspended as a divided country between two blocs given the lack of a post-1945 peace agreement. So there is a certain mournful symmetry in Britain's joining the ERM – after more than a decade of dithering – five days after the 3 October 1990 formalisation of German reunification in October. Despite a history and culture of separate development, Britain signed up to a central element of western European unity just at the time when it was changing force and character in a way that no one – certainly not the British with their island ways – could even recognise, let alone understand.

With the fall of the Berlin Wall and the dissolution of the Soviet empire, the circumstances that had drawn western Europe together after 1945 were starting to lose traction. Europe's political leaders (principally Helmut Kohl and François Mitterrand) believed transforming the Bundesbank-dominated ERM into economic and monetary union with a community-wide currency was an essential instrument both to complete European integration and to guard against German hegemony. Yet Britain climbed on board the ERM bandwagon at a singularly inappropriate time. The ignominy of joining the mechanism and subsequently mishandling it fell to the Conservatives, as a result of the abject failure of the Thatcher government's flagship counter-inflation policy, namely monetarism. The build-up to ERM membership provided an apt illustration of the Conservative party's historical practice of opportunistically shifting its ground and moving to new policy positions when established doctrines prove wanting.

In the early years of Thatcher's prime ministership, in 1979-81, inflation, instead of being brought under control by attempts to reduce the growth of the money supply, doubled. In addition, events in the foreign exchange market severely tested the faith of Thatcher and Nigel Lawson, her powerful second chancellor, in the wonders of market forces. What followed was a classic example of the influence of fashion on the search for a British economic policy panacea. For, as John Major ruefully reflected in his memoirs, in 1990 it was difficult to find anyone in the British political, financial and industrial establishment who was not in favour of entry to the ERM – in sharp contrast to the comments so many of these people made after the event.[2]

Intermingled with these developments were three tragic British miscalculations which became known gradually as Britain's ERM adventure unravelled. The first error was to underestimate how the EMU goal of a permanent currency merger was already a powerful influence (particularly for the French) over the ERM's operation. In the decisive months of July-September 1992, Britain was unable to use the flexibility in running the ERM that the UK government had believed was one of its prime tenets. The shadow of EMU (which most British ministers either opposed, had grave reservations over or believed would not happen) already lay over the ERM, in a way that few at the time realised.

Second, Britain failed to appreciate how Germany's reunification-induced economic overheating and the Bundesbank's associated desire to raise German interest rates would necessarily counter Britain's overriding objective of easing the credit squeeze in line with success in defeating inflation. The result of this conflict could only be an increased threat of a political and economic upheaval. After the 1991 Maastricht summit that sealed the single currency timetable, the mood turned vitriolic.

The inflationary consequences of German reunification, inflamed by the over-valuation of the East German Mark when it was replaced by the D-mark in July 1990, became increasingly evident. The crisis laid bare, at the Treasury but particularly at the Bank of England, grave shortcomings in awareness of Germany's monetary policy priorities. If, as has sometimes been rumoured, the UK intelligence agencies had a 'mole' in the Bundesbank during the 1980s and early 1990s, then any such source must have been grossly ill-informed or else some type of double agent.

Third, Prime Minister John Major wholly overestimated his ability to influence German monetary policies. Even set against past standards of other inept British attempts at European diplomacy over the decades, Major's three fruitless letters on interest rates to Kohl in July-August 1992, a bid to apply pressure on the Bundesbank via the German chancellor, stand out as prime examples of haplessness.

Kohl was indeed a central figure in a European nexus where, at every step, money, politics and power were intertwined. And – after a personal post-Black Wednesday intervention from François Mitterrand, with whom he had a dramatically more intense and emotional relationship than with any British prime minister – it is true that Kohl did telephone Helmut

Schlesinger and Hans Tietmeyer in Washington to browbeat the central bank into supporting the French franc. But to expect Kohl to intervene over interest rates on behalf of Britain was a crass form of wishful thinking. Major's predecessor, Margaret Thatcher, had fundamentally fallen out with Kohl over her uninhibited antipathy to reunification, where she displayed her misgivings far less subtly than Mitterrand.

France, Britain and Italy would have had a better chance of prevailing against the Bundesbank had they possessed the intelligence and strategic insight to join forces in 1991, soon after reunification, in seeking a German revaluation.

This would have pre-empted the exchange rate pressures that erupted in 1992, and mitigated the strains on individual countries having to decide whether to devalue. As it is, the build-up of European pleas (led noisily but ineffectively by the UK) for German interest rate cuts came when the issue of a possible currency realignment had already become hopelessly intermingled with France's September 1992 Maastricht referendum. These late, desperate efforts to break through the monetary impasse were doomed to failure.

The on-off history of Britain's ties with the ERM extends back to the 1970s. The litany of misjudgement over nearly 50 years forms a discouraging backcloth for Britain's struggle to negotiate terms for leaving the EU that will maintain and enhance the UK's trading relationships and keep faith with different factions of the powerful lobbies on different sides of the arguments. The shifting global environment – the dislocation stemming from President Donald Trump, the centrifugal and centripetal forces in Europe, China's political and financial campaign for greater world status – pose additional challenges.

Nothing epitomises the changing landscape better than Emmanuel Macron. The new French president, a mere 14 years old at the time of Black Wednesday, swept to victory in the May 2017 election by comprehensively defeating – for the moment at least – the forces of political 'populism'. The former economy minister, who had never previously held elected office, has taken office on a platform favouring economic reforms, greater co-operation with Germany and heightened European integration, aspiring to build on the foundations of the single currency to produce a much firmer political and economic union.

All this is a reminder of successive waves of pro-integrationist fervour in France and Germany which, in past decades, have foundered as a result of poor economic performance, external perturbations and insufficient application. This time it could be different. The UK's actions in sidelining itself from continental Europe – like the British decision to stand aside from the common market in the 1950s – has undoubtedly provided fresh impetus for Franco-German unity, with multiple implications across Europe. As the contortions of September 1992 recede into history, the European plot winds on. The tangled and tragicomic tale of Black Wednesday provides a warning of how great plans can go awry. For those who heed its lessons, the saga may help guide a path to more successful endeavour.

NOTES

Chapter One: 'Tool that broke in my hands'

1. HMT-FT-FoI. Andrew Holden note to Terry Burns, 'The Cost of Intervention', 10 December 1993.
2. Plenderleith telephone interview with Marsh, London, 16 June 2017.
3. David Kynaston, *The City of London: A Club No More, 1945-2000*, 2002, p.751.
4. Turnbull telephone interview with Marsh, London, 3 July 2017.
5. Lambert interview with Marsh, London, 14 June 2007.
6. Leigh-Pemberton interview with Marsh, 27 April 2007.
7. Major interview with Marsh, London, 26 September 2007.
8. Burns telephone interview with Marsh, London, 23 May 2017.
9. Lamont, *In Office*, 1999, p.244.
10. 'Quotes of the Day', *Financial Times*, 17 September 1992.
11. BBC transcript, 18 September 1992.
12. Kaletsky, 'Happy days are here again', *The Times*, 18 September 1992.
13. Schlesinger interview with Marsh, Oberursel, 2 July 2007.
14. *Financial Times*, 17 September 1992.
15. Major, *The Autobiography*, 1999.
16. William Keegan, 'Full marks to the Bundesbank', *The Observer*, 20 September 1992.
17. Jacques de Larosière, *50 Ans de crises financières*, 2016, p.155.
18. Lamont, *In Office*, 1999, p.266.
19. *Ibid.*, p.390.

Chapter Two: When George Soros won

1. Philip Stephens, *Politics and the Pound*, 1996, p.249.
2. Sebastian Mallaby, *More Money Than God: Hedge Funds and the Making of a New Elite*, 2010, p.22.
3. Daniel Capocci, *The Complete Guide to Hedge Funds & Hedge Fund Strategies*, 2013, pp.6-7
4. Carol Loomis, 'The Jones Nobody Keeps Up With', *Fortune*, April 1966.
5. Capocci, *The Complete Guide to Hedge Funds & Hedge Fund Strategies*, 2013, p.9.
6. Anise Wallace, 'The World's Greatest Money Manager', *Institutional Investor*, June 1981.
7. 'George Soros. It's done with mirrors', *The Economist*, 10 October 1987.
8. Mallaby, *More Money Than God: Hedge Funds and the Making of a New Elite*, 2010, p.148.
9. 'How we broke the Bank of England – Robert Johnson on Reality Asserts Itself', Real News Network, 12 June 2014.
10. Mallaby, *More Money Than God: Hedge Funds and the Making of a New Elite*, 2010, p.161.
11. Thomas Jaffe and Dyan Machan, 'How the Market Overwhelmed the Central Banks', *Forbes*, 9 November 1992.
12. Kaletsky, 'How Mr Soros made a billion by betting against the pound', *The Times*, 26 October 1992.
13. Jaffe and Machan, 'How the Market Overwhelmed the Central Banks', *Forbes*, 9 November 1992.
14. Kaletsky, 'How Mr Soros made a billion by betting against the pound', *The Times*, 26 October 1992.
15. Mallaby, *More Money Than God: Hedge Funds and the Making of a New Elite*, 2010, p.167.

16. Kaletsky, 'How Mr Soros made a billion by betting against the pound', *The Times*, 26 October 1992.
17. Jaffe and Machan, 'How the Market Overwhelmed the Central Banks', *Forbes*, 9 November 1992.
18. Alex Brummer, 'Governor seeks easier life after decade with Old Lady', *The Guardian*, 23 June 1993.

Chapter Three: Serial crises
1. Lamont, resignation speech, House of Commons, 9 June 1993.
2. Lamont was referring to Carlo Azeglio Ciampi, governor of the Banca d'Italia.
3. Reuven Glick and Michael Hutchinson, 'Currency Crises', Federal Reserve Bank of San Francisco Working Paper Series, WP2011-12, September 2011, p.2.
4. Michael Bordo, Barry Eichengreen, Daniela Klingebiel and Maria Soledad Martinez-Peria, 'Is the Crisis Problem Growing More Severe?', World Bank, December 2000, pp.36-40.
5. Richard Roberts, 'A Tremendous Panic': The Global Financial Crisis of 1914', in Andrew Smith, Simon Mollan, and Kevin D. Tennent, *The Impact of the First World War on International Business*, 2017, p.130.
6. Luc Laeven and Fabian Valencia, 'Systemic Banking Crises', in Stijin Claessens, M. Ayhan Kose, Luc Laeven and Fabian Valencia, *Financial Crises: Causes, Consequences, and Policy Responses*, IMF, 2014 pp.64-66; Paul Krugman, *Currency Crises*, 2000, p.1.
7. Paul Krugman, *Currency Crises*, 2000, p.1
8. See Glick and Hutchinson, 'Currency Crises'; Goldstein, Itay and Assaf Razin, 'Three Branches of Theories of Financial Crises', *Foundations and Trends in Finance, vol.10, no.2*, 2015 pp.154-167; Kaminsky, Graciela L., 'Varieties of Currency Crises', NBER Working Paper Series WP10193, 2003.
9. Krugman, *Currency Crises*, 2000, p.2.
10. *Ibid.*
11. *Ibid.*, p.3.
12. Razin, 'Three Branches of Theories of Financial Crises', *Foundations and Trends in Finance, vol.10, no.2*, 2015, p.162.
13. Stevens, 'The Asian Crisis: A Retrospective', Bulletin of the Reserve Bank of Australia, 2007, p.65.
14. Mallaby, *More Money Than God: Hedge Funds and the Making of a New Elite*, 2010, p.198.
15. Soros, *The Crisis of Global Capitalism*, 1998 p.143.
16. Peter Temple, *Hedge Funds: The Courtesans of Capitalism*, 2001, p.147.
17. *Financial Times*, 12-13 January 1998.
18. 'Where Was the IMF?', *Euromoney*, November 1992.
19. James Broughton, *Tearing Down Walls: The International Monetary Fund 1990-1999*, 2012, pp.23-24.
20. Richard Cooper, *Currency Devaluation in Developing Countries, Essays in International Finance, No.86*, 1971.
21. Jeffrey Frankel, 'Contractionary Currency Crashes in Developing Countries', The 5th Mundell-Fleming Lecture IMF Annual Research Conference, 2004.

Chapter Four: Nation apart
1. *The Collected Essays of Sir Winston Churchill, Volume II 'Churchill and Politics*, 1976, pp. 176-86.
2. Hugo Young, *This Blessed Plot: Britain and Europe from Churchill to Blair*, 2016.
3. Stephen Wall, *A Stranger in Europe*, 2008, pp. 204-09.
4. N.J. Crowson, *The Conservative Party and European Integration Since 1945: At the Heart of Europe?*, 2006.
5. See for example, Norman Davies, *God's Playground: A History of Poland*, 1979.
6. Churchill to de Gaulle, 4 June 1944; Charles de Gaulle, *War Memoirs: Unity 1942-44*, 1959.
7. Daniel Gros and Niels Thygesen, *European Monetary Integration*, 1998, p.4.
8. Michael D. Bordo, 'The Bretton Woods International Monetary System: A Historical Overview', in Michael D. Bordo and Barry Eichengreen, *A Retrospective on the Bretton Woods System*, 1993, p.49.
9. Gros and Thygesen, *European Monetary Integration*, 1998, p.9.

Chapter Five: 'This poor man'
1. De Gaulle address to French Cabinet, November 1962.
2. Blessing remarks, NDR radio, 27 January, 1963.
3. BoE, G1/188. Blessing letter to Cromer, 10 October 1962.

4. Chaban-Delmas speech to National Assembly, 26 June 1969
5. AAPD, Document 99, pp. 377–78. De Gaulle conversation with Kiesinger, Paris, March 1969.
6. Debré, *Mémoires: Gouverner autrement 1962-70*, 1993, p.325.
7. Werner et al, 'Report to the Council and the Commission on the Realisation by Stages of Economic and Monetary Union in the Community', Supplement to Bulletin II – 1970 of the European Communities, Brussels, Chapter III, p.10.
8. Willy Brandt, *Erinnerungen*, 1989, p.453, 1 December 1969.
9. BoE, 5A180/2. T.G. Underwood, 'European Economic and Monetary Integration: The Werner Report in Perspective', 1970.
10. HADB, N2/156. Brandt letter to Schiller, Bonn, 1970.
11. Harold James, *International Monetary Cooperation Since Bretton Woods*, 1996, p.239.
12. Robert Solomon, *The International Monetary System 1945-1976*, 1977, p.221.
13. Forrest Capie, *The Bank of England 1950's-1979*, 2010.

Chapter Six: Europe of many dimensions
1. Marjolin, *Architect of European Unity, Memoirs 1911-86*, 1989, p.364.
2. HADB, B330/9942. Klasen letter to Brandt, Frankfurt, 3 October 1973.
3. UKNA, PREM 15/1564. Conversation, Chequers, after dinner, 6 October 1973.
4. Giscard radio address, Paris, West German government statement, Bonn, 19 January 1974.
5. Giscard d'Estaing, *Macht und Leben*, 1988, p.122.
6. Barry Eichengreen, *Globalizing Capital: A History of the International Monetary System*, 2008 p.150.
7. HADB, N2/264. 'Personal' Pöhl letter to Schmidt, Frankfurt, 21 March 1978.
8. Keegan attended the press conference on 17 July 1978 on behalf of *The Observer*.
9. Dell, *A Strange Eventful History: Democratic Socialism in Britain*, 1999.
10. Healey interview with Marsh, Alfriston, 10 April 2007.
11. Healey, *The Time of my Life*, 1989.
12. Lahnstein interview with Marsh, Hamburg, 10 June 2007.
13. James, *International Monetary Cooperation Since Bretton Woods*, 1996, p.475.
14. Emminger, evidence to Treasury and Civil Service Committee, House of Commons, 1982.
15. Gros and Thygesen, *European Monetary Integration*, 1998, pp.162-63.
16. Eichengreen, *Globalizing Capital: A History of the International Monetary System, 2008*, p.160.
17. IFM, Meeting between Mitterrand and Kohl, 4 October 1982.
18. Thatcher, *The Downing Street Years*, 1993, p.553.
19. IFM, Mitterrand conversaton with Kissinger, Paris, 28 June 1984.
20. André Gauron interview with Marsh, Paris, 29 May 2007.
21. Eichengreen, *Globalizing Capital: A History of the International Monetary System, 2008*, pp.162-64.
22. Adam Raphael, *The Observer's* political editor, attended the briefing.
23. Keegan, *Mr Lawson's Gamble*, 1989, p.181. Lawson, *The View from No.11*, 1992, p.499.
24. André Szász, *The Road to Monetary Union*, 1999, p.93.
25. Tietmeyer, *Herausforderung Euro*, 2005, p.47.
26. Lawson, *The View from No.11*, 1992, p.500.
27. *Ibid.*, pp.655-56.
28. Lawson interview with Marsh, London, 30 April 2007.

Chapter Seven: Shadow of the D-mark
1. Thatcher statement, 10 June 1986.
2. Private information.
3. Lawson, evidence to Treasury Select Committee, 9 December 1987.
4. *The Observer*, 15 March 1987.
5. *Ibid.*, 26 March 1987.
6. Thatcher parliamentary answer, 1988.
7. Lawson, *The View from No.11*, 1992, p.955.
8. Genscher interview with Marsh, Pech, 5 October 2007.
9. Harold James, *Making the European Monetary Union*, p.229. HADB., B330/17837. 1 May 1998, Bundesbank council meeting.
10. Lawson, *The View from No.11*, 1992, pp.917-26, 927-36.
11. *Ibid.*, 1992, pp.902-03.
12. Delors, *Mémoires*, p.334.

13. HADB, ZBR 753. 30 June 1988.
14. BoE. 8A/250/1. J. Footman, Delors committee, 4 July 1988.
15. HADB, ZBR 754. 14 July 1988.
16. Gros and Thygesen, *European Monetary Integration, 1998*, p.69.
17. Stephens, *Politics and the Pound*, 1996, pp.76-87.
18. Thatcher, interview with BBC World Service, 19 May 1989.
19. Pöhl interview with Marsh, Frankfurt, 9 May 2007.
20. UKNA, PREM. 19/2967. Delors Committee Note from Lawson to Thatcher, 13 February 1989. Letter from Leigh-Pemberton to Thatcher, 17 February 1989. Note from Powell to Thatcher, 17 February 1989.
21. Thatcher, *The Downing Street Years*, 1993, pp.709-13.

Chapter Eight: Reluctant convert
1. Lawson resignation letter to Thatcher, 27 October 1989.
2. Private information.
3. Susan Howson, *Lionel Robbins*, 2011, p.248.
4. Major, parliamentary debate, 31 October, 1989.
5. Major interview with Marsh, London, 26 September 2007.
6. Heath, House of Commons, 29 November 1988; *Lawson, The View from No.11*, 1992, pp.847-48.
7. Major, Statement European Council meeting, Edinburgh, 12 December 1992.
8. Thatcher speech, European Parliament, 1986.
9. *Financial Times*, 11 July 1990.
10. Major lecture, London School of Economics and Political Science, 24 April 2007.
11. Leigh-Pemberton interview with Marsh, 27 April 2007.
12. UKNA, PREM. Anglo-German Relations. Thatcher-Genscher meeting between at 10 Downing Street, 30 July 1990. Letter from Powell to Wall, 30 July 1990. BBPO-GU. No. 222, p.439

Chapter Nine: In the dark
1. Treasury and Civil Service Committee, 25 July 1990.
2. BoE, 4A/99-1. Note from Andrew Crockett, 20 August 1990. ERM Entry: The exchange rate and interest rates. Note from Anthony Coleby, 30 August 1990.
3. BoE, 14A/99-1. Minutes of a meeting, HM Treasury on Friday 31 August 1990.
4. BoE, 414A/990-1. Governor's bilateral with the Chancellor of the Exchequer, 6 September 1990.
5. Keegan, 25-27 September 1990, *The Observer*.
6. Baker, *The Turbulent Years: My Life in Politics,* 1993.
7. George interview with Marsh, 8 April 2008.
8. BoE, 14A/99-1. Letter from Burns.
9. *Ibid.* Letter from Leigh-Pemberton to Thatcher (with copy to Major), 4 October 1990.
10. *Ibid.* Letter from Andrew Turnbull, Thatcher's principal private secretary, to John Gieve (Treasury), 4 October 1990.
11. UKNA, CAB 128/97. Conclusions of Cabinet meeting, 10 Downing Street, 4 October 1990.
12. Lamont, *In Office*, 1999, p.8.
13. BoE, 14A 99/1.
14. Howe, *Conflict of Loyalty*, 1994, p.639.
15. UKNA, CAB 128/97. Conclusions of Cabinet meeting, 10 Downing Street, Thursday 18 October 1990.

Chapter Ten: Taking the plunge
1. BoE, 14A 99/1. Note for record by C B Briault, deputy governor's office. 'ERM entry: conversations on 5 October 1990'.
2. *Ibid.*
3. Tietmeyer, *Herausforderung Euro*, 2005.
4. BoE, 14A/99-1. Note by T. Tarkowski to Nigel Wicks, 5 October 1990.
5. UKNA, CAB 128/97. Conclusions of Cabinet meeting, 10 Downing Street, Thursday 18 October 1990.
6. Delors, *Mémoires*, p.423.
7. Tietmeyer interview with Marsh, Königstein, 10 May 2007.
8. HMT-DM-FoI. 'Should sterling rejoin and if so when?', From A Turnbull to Chancellor of the Exchequer, 18 September 1992.
9. HMT-FT-FoI. Nigel Wicks, 'Reflections on the UK's membership of the ERM', 1994.

Chapter Eleven: Hot seat
1. *Financial Times*, 8 October 1992.
2. Major, London Weekend TV's Walden's World interview, 7 October 1992.
3. Smith response to Major statement, House of Commons, 15 October 1990.
4. ERM Witness Seminar, organised by Centre for Contemporary British History, Churchill Archives Centre and Lombard Street Research, 14 November 2007.
5. Howe resignation speech to House of Commons, 13 November, 1990.
6. Major speech in Bonn, 11 March 1991.
7. Lamont, *In Office*, 1999, p.8.
8. Keegan, 'Mr Lamont's dark history', *The Observer*, 22 July 2007.
9. *Ibid.*
10. Lamont speech to European Policy Forum, London, 10 July 1992.
11. HMT-FT-FoI. 'Britain and the exchange rate mechanism – Chancellor's speech to the European Policy Forum', 29 July 1993.

Chapter Twelve: 'Against German interests'
1. UKNA, PREM 19/2185, Anglo-German Summit, Downing Street background paper, attached to letter of 18 September 1986.
2. Jacques Attali, *Verbatim III*, 6 December 1989.
3. BKA-DE, No.120, p. 638, Talks between Baker and Kohl, West Berlin, 12 December 1989.
4. IFM, Elysée palace transcript, Mitterrand conversation with Thatcher, Paris, 20 January 1990.
5. Kohl statement to Bundestag, 15 February 1990.
6. Marsh, 'The D-mark crosses the wall', *Financial Times*, 16 February 1990.
7. HMT-FT-FoI. Stephen Davies, ERM project paper-'The safest conclusion is that a period of turbulence for the DM cannot be ruled out.'
8. HMT-FT-FoI. 'Reflections on the UK's membership of the ERM', Note from Paul Gray to Terry Burns, 5 January 1994.
9. DPBO Minute from Charles Powell to Thatcher, 9 February 1990.
10. In November 1990 Pöhl asked Kohl to freeze government spending. In January 1991 Schlesinger warned publicly on the need for ERM realignments. In March 1991 Pöhl made unguarded comments in Brussels on the 'disaster' caused by Kohl's reunification policies.
11. The Bundesbank had never previously raised rates with such intensity in August, although it did decide 0.5 percentage point increases in discount rate in early to mid-August in 1955 and 1965.
12. Schlesinger interview with Marsh, Frankfurt, 14 February 2007.
13. Bank for International Settlements Annual Report, 1993, p.183.
14. *Financial Times*, 12 March 1991.
15. Maastricht treaty, articles 101, 103 and 116.
16. Schlesinger interview with Marsh, Oberursel, 2 July 2007.
17. Wager with Marsh, Maastricht, 9 December 1991. Kohl letter to Marsh, 3 February 1997.
18. Éric Aeschimann and Pascal Riché, *La Guerre de Sept Ans*, 1996, p.137.
19. IFM. Guillaume Hanezzo note to Mitterrand, Paris, 18 December 1991.
20. Lubbers letter to Kohl, 15 January 1992.

Chapter Thirteen: Grumbling volcano
1. Leigh-Pemberton speech, Tokyo, 8 October 1992.
2. Lamont, *In Office*, 1999, p.198.
3. Major interview with Marsh, London, 26 September 2007.
4. Bérégovoy speech, National Assembly, Paris, 5 May 1992.
5. Bérégovoy comments, French TV debate, May 1992.
6. McDougall article, *The Observer*, 22 March 1992.
7. *Financial Times*, 4 June 1992.
8. *Ibid.*, 21 May 1992.
9. *Süddeutsche Zeitung*, 19 May 1992.
10. *Frankfurter Allgemeine Zeitung*, 11 June 1992.
11. Lamberto Dini interview with Marsh, Rome, 26 June 2007.
12. NYFA, CF. Foreign Exchange 100260. Ted Truman (Federal Reserve Board) note to Alan-Greenspan, 5 June 1992, reporting on telephone conversations with Rieke and Crockett on the European Monetary Committee meeting, 3 June 1992.
13. Spencer, 'The UK economy, Lost in the Black Forest', Kleinwort Benson Research, June 1992.
14. HMT-FT-FoI. Stephen Davies, 'ERM Project paper', 21 December 1993.

15. Tietmeyer, *Herausforderung Euro,* 2005, p.178.
16. Lamont, *In Office,* 1999, pp.211-13.
17. Major, *The Autobiography,* 1999, pp.315-16.
18. HADB, B330/24145. Report on council meeting, 16 July 1992.
19. IFM, French Cabinet papers, 22 July 1992.

Chapter Fourteen: Hint of sabotage
1. HADB, 330/24146. Report on Bundesbank council meeting, 6 August 1992. B330/24147. Report on Bundesbank council meeting, 20 August 1992.
2. HMT-FT-FoI. Stephen Davies, 'ERM project paper', 21 December 1993, p.81.
3. Lamont, *In Office,* 1999, p.225.
4. *Financial Times,* 25 August 1992.
5. 'Forever falling?', *The Economist,* 29 August 1992.
6. Lex, 'D-Day for the dollar', *Financial Times,* 22 August 1992.
7. Lamont, *In Office,* 1999, p.222.
8. *Ibid.,* p.228.
9. *Financial Times,* 27 August 1992.
10. IFM. French presidential transcript, Kohl-Mitterrand meeting, Borkum, 26 August 1992.
11. *The Times,* 27 August 1992.
12. Stephens, *Politics and the Pound, 1996,* p.216.
13. Tietmeyer, interview with Marsh, Königstein, 10 May 2007.
14. Lamont interview with Marsh, London, 2 April 2007. Lamont, *In Office,* p.228.
15. HMT-DM-FoI. Heywood note to Norman Lamont. Chex.jp/jh/55. 'Contingency measures - You may welcome some thoughts on a contingency package.'
16. Major, *The Autobiography,* 1999, p.320, Tietmeyer, *Herausforderung Euro,* p.181.
17. Amato interview with Marsh, Rome/London, 28 June 2007.
18. Major, *The Autobiography,* 1999 pp. 320-25.
19. *Ibid.*
20. *Ibid.*
21. Waigel interview with Marsh, Munich, 17 April 2007.
22. Tietmeyer interview with Marsh, Königstein, 10 May 2007.
23. Major interview with Marsh, London, 26 September 2007.
24. HADA, B330/24148/1. Report on Bundesbank council, 3 September 1992. Foreign exchange market report. 2 September 1992.
25. 'No retreat for inflation buster', *Financial Times,* 29 August 1992.
26. Major, *The Autobiography,* 1999, p.321.
27. HADA, B330/24148/1. Report on Bundesbank council meeting, 3 September 1992.
28. Lamont, *In Office,* 1999, pp.233-38.
29. Leigh-Pemberton interview with Marsh, 27 April 2007.
30. Kok interview with Marsh, Amsterdam, 2 October 2007.
31. Private information.
32. Lamont interview with Marsh, London, 2 April 2007.
33. Clarke interview with Marsh, London, 11 March 2008.
34. Transcript of Lamont press conference, Bath, 5 September 1992.
35. Dini interview with Marsh, Rome, 26 June 2007.
36. Major speech to Scottish CBI, Glasgow, 10 September 1992.

Chapter Fifteen: Weekend manoeuvering
1. *The Times,* 11 September 1992.
2. Carlo Azeglio Ciampi, Banca d'Italia governor, remarks to parliamentary committee, Rome, 10 September 1992.
3. Bank for International Settlements 1983 Annual Report, p.188.
4. HADB, N2/267. Emminger letter to Schmidt, 16 November 1978.
5. HADB, N2/267. Transcript. Bundesbank council, 30 November 1978.
6. *Handelsblatt* report, December 1978
7. Joachim Bitterlich, unpublished manuscript, 'Beobachtungen und Anmerkungen eines Zeitzeugen über vier Jahrzehnte erlebter deutscher und europäischer Geschichte – eine Hommage an Helmut Kohl', June 2017.
8. Amato interview with Marsh, Rome/London, 16 June 2017.
9. Tietmeyer diary, 11 September 1992.

10. HADB, B330/24149. Account of 11 September meeting, related at Bundesbank council meeting of 14 September 1992.
11. Tietmeyer interview with Marsh, Königstein, 10 May 2007.
12. Schlesinger interview with Marsh, Oberursel, 2 July 2007.
13. Sapin interview with Marsh, Paris, 3 October 2007.
14. Waigel interview with Marsh, Munich, 7 April 2007.
15. Dini interview with Marsh, Rome, 26 June 2007.
16. Lamont, *In Office*, 1999, p.265.
17. Barucci telephone interview with Marsh, Rome/London, 11 October 2007.
18. Stephens, *Politics and the Pound*, 1996, p.239.
19. Major interview with Marsh, London, 26 September 2007.
20. Major, *The Autobiography*, 1999, p.326.
21. Amato interview with Marsh, Rome/London, 28 June 2007.
22. Harold James, *Making the European Monetary Union*, p.357.
23. Saccomanni interview with Marsh, Rome, 26 June 2007.
24. Smith, 'Euro doom - Maastricht treaty', *Sunday Times*, 13 September 1992.
25. Marshall, 'Europe on the brink - Maastricht and EMS at break point', *Independent on Sunday*, 13 September 1992.

Chapter Sixteen: Schlesinger's message
1. Mitterrand remarks in TV debate on Maastricht referendum, 3 September 1992.
2. 'Shake-up alters shape of politics', *Financial Times*, 14 September 1992.
3. Private information.
4. HADA, B330/24149. Bundesbank council meeting, 14 September 1992.
5. Trott interview with Roberts, London, 3 May 2017.
6. The meeting, which was kept secret at the time, was first revealed by Samuel Brittan in the *Financial Times* on 21 January 1993. See Stephens, *Politics and the Pound*, p.240.
7. BoE, 9A/376/2. See James, *Making the European Monetary Union*, p.355.
8. Exchange Rate Mechanism: Black Wednesday and the Rebirth of the British Economy, Lombard Street Seminar, 14 November 2007.
9. Budd interview with Marsh, London, 25 September 2007.
10. Issing interview with Marsh, Frankfurt, 19 June 2017.
11. Schlesinger interview with Marsh, Oberusel, 2 July 2007.
12. 'EWS-Spannungen nicht endgültig gelöst', *Handelsblatt*, 16 September 1992. See also Bundesbank documentation on ERM crisis, Schlesinger letter to members of Bundesbank Council, 9 October 1992.
13. 'Inside story. The breaking of the pound', *Independent on Sunday*, 20 September 1992.
14. Werner Benkhoff, 'Zinssenkung war Angebot der Deutschen Bundesbank', *Handelsblatt*, 17 September 1992.
15. Schlesinger interview with Marsh, Oberursel, 2 July 2007.
16. Statement by Bill Robinson, Lombard Street Seminar, 14 November 2007.
17. Budd interview with Marsh, London, 25 September 2007.

Chapter Seventeen: Swimming against a tidal wave
1. Wall interview with Marsh, London, 18 June 2007.
2. 'The moment they knew the game was lost', *Evening Standard*, 17 September 1992.
3. *Ibid.*
4. Lamont, *In Office,* 1999, p.246.
5. *Ibid.*, p.247.
6. *Ibid.*
7. 'John Major's days of pain', *Sunday Times*, 20 September 1992.
8. 'The moment they knew the game was lost', *Evening Standard*, 17 September 1992.
9. 'A turbulent day in Whitehall', *Financial Times*, 17 September 1992.
10. Stephens, *Politics and the Pound,* 1996, p.248.
11. Hurd, *Memoirs*, 2003, pp.468-469.
12. 'Inside story. The breaking of the pound', *Independent on Sunday*, 20 September 1992.
13. Budd interview with Marsh, 25 September 2007.
14. Lamont, *In Office,* 1999, p.252.
15. Stephens, *Politics and the Pound,* 1996, p.249.
16. Lamont, *In Office,* p.248.

17. Stephens, *Politics and the Pound,* 1996, p.250.
18. Major, *The Autobiography*, 1999, p.330.
19. 'Inside story. The breaking of the pound', *Independent on Sunday*, 20 September 1992.
20. 'Sell, sell, sell', *The Guardian*, 17 September 1992.
21. 'John Major's days of pain', *Sunday Times*, 20 September 1992.
22. 'The moment they knew the game was lost', *Evening Standard*, 17 September 1992.
23. 'Inside story. The breaking of the pound', *Independent on Sunday*, 20 September 1992.
24. 'Quotes of the day', *Financial Times*, 17 September 1992.
25. Lamont, *In Office*, 1999, p.249.
26. Major, *The Autobiography*, 1999, p.331.
27. Lamont, *In Office*, 1999, p.249.
28. *Ibid.*, Major, *The Autobiography*, 1999, pp.330-31.
29. Major, *The Autobiography*, 1999, p.331.
30. 'Inside story. The breaking of the pound', *Independent on Sunday*, 20 September 1992.
31. Lamont, *In Office*, 1999, p.250.
32. Stephens, *Politics and the Pound,* 1996, p.251.
33. Lamont, *In Office*, 1999, p.252.
34. Hurd, *Memoirs*, 2003, pp.468-69.
35. Lamont, *In Office*, 1999, p.252.
36. Major, *The Autobiography*, 1999, p.332.
37. Lamont, *In Office*, 1999, p.252.
38. 'Inside story. The breaking of the pound', *Independent on Sunday*, 20 September 1992.
39. Burns interview with Marsh, 23 May 2017.
40. Clarke interview with Marsh, London, 11 March 2008.
41. Lamont, *In Office*, 1999, p.252.
42. *Ibid.*, p.253.
43. 'Sell, sell, sell', *The Guardian*, 17 September 1992.
44. *Ibid.*
45. 'Traders get warm glow from hot money', *Sunday Times*, 20 September 1992.
46. 'The ERM and Britain', *Financial Times*, 17 September 1992.
47. 'Shares rebound from 80-point loss', *The Times*, 17 September 1992.
48. Trott interview with Roberts, London, 3 May 2017.
49. Major interview with Marsh, London, 26 September 2007.
50. IFM. French Cabinet meeting, 16 September 1992.
51. Major, *The Autobiography*, 1999, p.332.
52. Wall interview with Marsh, London, 18 June 2007.
53. 'Inside story. The breaking of the pound', *Independent on Sunday*, 20 September 1992.
54. Tietmeyer, *Herausforderung Euro*, 2005, p.188.
55. Lamont, *In Office*, 1999, p.255.
56. Stephens, *Politics and the Pound,* 1996, p.247.
57. *Ibid.*, p.254.
58. 'Sterling crisis – how Major and Lamont lost the battle for the pound', *The Observer*, 20 September 1992.
59. HMT-DM-FoI. Cex/kf/jh2/24. 'Cabinet speaking notes.'
60. HMT-FT-FoI. 'Should sterling rejoin and if so when?', Turnbull note to Burns, 18 September 1992. HMT-DM-FoI. 'Should sterling rejoin and if so when?'. From A Turnbull to Chancellor of the Exchequer, 18 September 1992
61. *Financial Times*, 2 October 1992.
62. Exchange Rate Mechanism: Black Wednesday and the Rebirth of the British Economy, Lombard Street Seminar, 14 November 2007.
63. IFM. Elysée Palace note by Jean Vidal, Paris, 2 November 1992, on French Ambassador Bertrand Dufourq's conversation on 1 November 1992 with Schlesinger.
64. Budd, *A Re-examination of Britain's Experience in the Exchange Rate Mechanism*, 2005.

Chapter Eighteen: Field of ruins

1. Bitterlich, unpublished manuscript, 'Beobachtungen und Anmerkungen eines Zeitzeugen über vier Jahrzehnte erlebter deutscher und europäischer Geschichte – eine Hommage an Helmut Kohl', June 2017.
2. IFM. Account of Mitterrand-Kohl meeting, Paris, 22 September 1992.
3. *Ibid.*

4. IFM. 'Compete rendu des entretiens franco-allemands, mardi après-midi, 22 septembre, Washington.'
5. *Ibid.*
6. Tietmeyer, *Herausforderung Euro*, 2005.
7. Sapin interview with Marsh, Paris, 3 October 2007.
8. Hannezo note to Mitterrand, Paris, 23 September 1992.
9. Jean Vidal note, Paris, 3 October 1992.
10. IFM. Conversation Major-Mitterrand, Paris, 30 September 1992, Elysée palace transcript.
11. IFM. Trichet personal memorandum, Paris, 11 December 1992.
12. Balludur letter to Kohl, 29 July 1993.
13. Tietmeyer, *Herausforderung Euro*, 2005, pp.205-12.
14. De Larosière interview with Marsh, Paris, 28 June 2007.
15. Clarke interview with Marsh, London, 11 March 2008.
16. Balludur interview with Marsh, Paris, 29 May 2007.
17. IFM. French Cabinet meeting, Paris, 4 August 1993.
18. Noyer interview with Marsh, Paris, 27 June 2007.

Chapter Nineteen: Lightning conductor

1. Keegan, 'Mr Lamont's dark history', *The Observer,* 22 July 2007.
2. Lamont, *In Office,* 1999, p.264.
3. Lamont interview with Marsh, London, 2 April 2007.
4. Lamont letter to John Watts, chairman, House of Commons Treasury Committee, 8 October 1992.
5. Lamont resignation speech, House of Commons, 9 June 1993.
6. Smith reply to Lamont resignation speech, House of Commons, 9 June 1993.
7. Budd, *A Re-examination of Britain's Experience in the Exchange Rate Mechanism*, 2005.
8. Keegan, *The Observer*, 17 June 2007.
9. Clarke interview with Keegan, *The Observer*, 7 October 2007.

Chapter Twenty: Shock and survival

1. Schlesinger, 'Money is just the start', *The Economist,* 21 September 1996.
2. Issing comments at conference, Hamburg, November 2007.
3. Tietmeyer speech, Aachen, 3 November 1997.
4. European Commission, Economic and Financial Affairs, 'Myths and facts', 30 April 2009,
5. 'Strong euro hid crisis, says EU chief', *Financial Times,* 14 June 2010.
6. Delors speech, Brussels, 28 March 2012.
7. Draghi speech, Shanghai, 3 June 2013.

Chapter Twenty One: First and second Brexit

1. Churchill, speech to House of Commons, 4 June 1940.
2. Major, *The Autobiography*, 1999.

SOURCES

Archives

Germany

Deutsche Bundesbank (Historisches Archiv) (HADB)

Federal Chancellery (Bundeskanzleramt), *Dokumente zur Deutschlandpolitik: Deutsche Einheit – Sonderedition aus den Akten des Bundeskanzleramtes 1989/90*, R. Oldenbourg Verlag, eds, Hans Jürgen Küsters and Daniel Hofmann, Munich (BKA-DE)

Federal Ministry of Foreign Affairs (Auswärtiges Amt), Akten zur Außenpolitik der Bundesrepublik Deutschland, Institut für Zeitgeschichte, Berlin (AAPD)

France

Institut François Mitterrand (IFM), including *Mitterrand et la réunification allemande – Une histoire secrète 1981–1995*, Thilo Schabert, Paris

UK

Bank of England Archives, London (BoE)

HM Treasury, Freedom of Information Act, *Financial Times* documents 2005 (HMT-FT-FoI), David Marsh documents (HMT-DM-FoI)

Documents on British Policy Overseas, Foreign and Commonwealth Office, London (DBPO)

National Archives, Kew (UKNA)

US

National Archives, Washington (USNA)

Federal Reserve Bank of New York Archives, New York (NYFA)

Books and articles

Aeschimann, Eric and Riché, Pascal, *La Guerre de Sept Ans* (Paris: Calmann-Lévy, 1996)

Apel, Emmanuel, *European Monetary Integration: 1958-2002* (London: Routledge, 1998)

Attali, Jacques, *Verbatim III, Deuxième partie 1990–91* (Paris: Fayard, 1996)

Baker, Kenneth, *The Turbulent Years: My Life in Politics* (London: Faber and Faber 1993)

Bank of England, 'Policy after the ERM; supervision after Bingham', Bank of England Quarterly Bulletin (Q4 November 1992) 458-60

Bank for International Settlements, 63rd Annual Report, Chap. VIII: 'Foreign Exchange Markets: developments and their possible causes' (Basel, 1993) 182-200

Bitterlich, Joachim, 'Beobachtungen und Anmerkungen eines Zeitzeugen über vier Jahrzehnte erlebter deutscher und europäischer Geschichte – eine Hommage an Helmut Kohl', June 2017

Bordo, Michael D., 'The Bretton Woods International Monetary System: A Historical Overview', in Bordo, Michael D. and Eichengreen, Barry (eds), *A Retrospective on the Bretton Woods System* (Chicago: University of Chicago Press, 1993)

Bordo, Michael D. and Schwartz, Anna J., 'Why Clashes Between Internal and External Stability Goals End in Currency Crises, 1797-1994' NBER Working Papers Series WP5710 (August 1996)

Bordo, Michael and Jonung, Lars, *Lessons for EMU from the History of Monetary Unions* (London: IEA, 2000)

Bordo, Michael, Eichengreen, Barry, Klingebiel, Daniela and Martinez-Peria, Maria Soledad, *Is the Crisis Problem Growing More Severe?* (Washington DC: World Bank, December 2000)

Brandt, Willy, *Erinnerungen* (Berlin: Ullstein Tb, 1989)

Broughton, James, *Tearing Down Walls: The International Monetary Fund 1990-1999* (Washington DC: IMF, 2012)

Budd, Alan, *Black Wednesday: A Re-examination of Britain's Experience in the Exchange Rate Mechanism* (London: IEA, 2005)

Buiter, Willem H., Corsetti, Giancarlo M., and Pesenti, Paolo A., *Financial markets and European monetary cooperation: The Lessons of the 1992-93 Exchange Rate Mechanism crisis* (New York: Cambridge University Press, 1998)

Buiter, Willem H., Corsetti, Giancarlo M., and Pesenti, Paolo A., 'Interpreting the ERM crisis: country-specific and systemic issues', Princeton Studies in International Finance No.84 (March 1998)

Capie, Forrest, *The Bank of England 1950's -1979* (Cambridge: Cambridge University Press, 2010)

Capocci, Daniel, T*he Complete Guide to Hedge Funds & Hedge Fund Strategies* (Basingstoke: Palgrave, 2013)

CCBH Witness Programme and Lombard Street Research, Exchange Rate Mechanism: Black Wednesday and the Rebirth of the British Economy (CCBH, 2008)

Churchill, Winston, *The Collected Essays of Sir Winston Churchill, Volume II 'Churchill and Politics'* (London: Library of Imperial History, 1976)

Cobham, David (eds), *European Monetary Upheavals* (Manchester: Manchester University Press, 1994)

Coffey, Peter and John R. Presley, *European Monetary Integration* (London: Macmillan, 1971)

Connolly, Bernard, *The Rotten Heart of Europe: The Dirty War for Europe's Money* (London: Faber and Faber, 1995)

Cooper, Richard N., Currency Devaluation in Developing Countries, Essays in International Finance, No.86 (Princeton NJ: International Finance Section, Department of Economics, Princeton University, 1971)

Crowson, N.J., *The Conservative Party and European Integration Since 1945: At the Heart of Europe?* (London: Routledge, 2006)

Davies, Norman, *God's Playground, A History of Poland* (New York: Columbia University Press, 1979)

Debré, Michel, *Mémoires: Gouverner Autrement*, 1962-70 (Paris: Albin Michel, 1993)

De Gaulle, Charles, *War Memoirs: Unity 1942* (New York: Simon and Schuster, 1959)

Dell, Edmund, *A Strange Eventful History: Democratic Socialism in Britain* (London: HarperCollins, 1999)

Delors, Jacques, *Mémoires* (Paris: PLON, 2004)

Dyson, Kenneth, *Elusive Union: The Process of Economic and Monetary Union in Europe* (London: Longman, 1994)

Edison, Hali J. and Kole, Linda S., 'European Monetary Arrangements: Implications for the Dollar, Exchange Rate Variability and Credibility', Federal Reserve System International Finance Discussion Papers no.468 (May 1994)

Eichengreen, Barry and Wyplosz, Charles, 'The Unstable EMS', Brookings Papers on Economic Activity, (no.1 1993) 51-143.

Eichengreen, Barry, 'The EMS Crisis in Retrospect', NBER Working Paper Series WP 8035 (December 2000)

Eichengreen, Barry, *The European Economy Since 1945* (Princeton NJ: Princeton University Press, 2007)

Eichengreen, Barry, *Globalizing Capital: A History of the International Monetary System* (Princeton NJ: Princeton New Jersey, 2008)

Frankel, Jeffrey, 'Contractionary Currency Crashes in Developing Countries', The 5th Mundell-Fleming Lecture IMF Annual Research Conference (2004)

Fratianni, Michele and Michele J Artis, 'The Lira and the Pound in the 1992 Currency Crisis: Fundamentals or Speculation?' Open Economies Review, vol.7 (1996) 573-589

Funke, Norbert, 'Vulnerability of Fixed Exchange Rate Regimes: The Role of Economic Fundamentals', OECD Economic Studies, no.26 (1996) 157-176

Giavazzi, Francesco and Giovannini, Alberto, *Limiting Exchange Rate Flexibility: The European Monetary System* (London: MIT Press, 1989)

Giovannini, Alberto and Mayer, Coli (ed), *European Financial Integration* (Cambridge: Cambridge University Press, 1991)

Giscard d'Estaing, Valéry, *Macht und Leben* (Berlin: Ullstein, 1988)

Glick, Reuven and Hutchinson, Michael, 'Currency Crises', Federal Reserve Bank of San Francisco Working Paper Series WP2011-12 (September 2011)

Goldstein, Itay and Razin, Assaf, 'Three Branches of Theories of Financial Crises', Foundations and Trends in Finance, vol.10, no.2 (2015)

Gros, Daniel and Thygesen, Neils, *European Monetary Integration* (London: Pearson, 1998)

Harmon, Mark D and Heisenberg, Dorothee, 'Explaining the European Currency Crisis of September 1992', German Politics & Society, No. 29, Germany in the New European Order (Summer 1993) 19-51

Healey, Denis, *The Time of My Life* (York: Methuen Publishing 1989)

Higgins, Byron, 'Was the ERM Crisis Inevitable?' Federal Reserve Bank of Kansas Economic Review (Q4 1993) 27-40.

Howe, Geoffrey, *Conflict of Loyalty* (London: Pan, 1995)

Howson, Susan, *Lionel Robbins* (Cambridge: Cambridge University Press, 2011)

Hurd, Douglas, *Memoirs* (London: Abacus, 2003)

IMF, World Economic Outlook, Chap III: 'Recent Changes in the European Exchange Rate Mechanism' (October 1993) 29-47

Ingham, Barbara, *International Economics: A European Focus* (London: FT Prentice Hall, 2004)

James, Harold, *International Monetary Cooperation Since Bretton Woods* (Oxford: Oxford University Press, 1996)

James, Harold, *Making the European Monetary Union* (Massachusetts: Harvard University Press, 2012)

Junor, Penny, *John Major: From Brixton to Downing Street* (London: Michael Joseph, 1996)

Kaminsky, Graciela L., 'Varieties of Currency Crises', NBER Working Paper Series WP10193 (December 2003)

Kenen, Peter B., *Economic and Monetary Union in Europe: Moving beyond Maastricht* (Cambridge: Cambridge University Press, 1995)

Krause, Lawrence B. and Salant, Walter S. (eds), *European Monetary Unification: and Its Meaning for the United States* (Washington D.C.: The Brookings Institution, 1973)

Krugman, Paul, *Currency Crises* (Chicago: University of Chicago Press, 2000)

Kynaston, David, *The City of London: A Club No More 1945-2000* (London: Chatto, 2002)

Laeven, Luc and Valencia, Fabian, 'Systemic Banking Crises', in Stijin Claessens, M. Ayhan Kose, Laeven, Luc and Valencia, Fabian, *Financial Crises: Causes, Consequences, and Policy Responses* (Washington DC: IMF, 2014)

Lamont, Norman, *In Office* (London: Warner, 1999)

Lamont, Norman, 'Black Wednesday — the Controversy Continues,' Central Banking vol.10 (1999-2000) 65-9.

Lawson, Nigel, *The View From No.11: Memoirs of a Tory Radical* (London: Bantam, 1992)

Lieberman, Sima, *The Long Road to a European Monetary Union* (London: University Press of America, 1992)

Magnifico, Giovanni, *European Monetary Unification* (London: Macmillan, 1973)

Mallaby, Sebastian, *More Money Than God: Hedge Funds and the Making of a New Elite* (London: Bloomsbury, 2010)

Major, John, *John Major, the Autobiography* (London: Harper Collins, 1999)

Marsh, David, *The Euro: The Battle for the New Global Currency* (London: Yale, 2009)

Marjolin, Robert, *Architect of European Unity, Memoirs 1911-86* (London: Weidenfeld and Nicolson, 1989)

Neal, Larry, *The Economics of Europe and the European Union* (Cambridge: Cambridge University Press, 2007)

Ozkan, F.G. and Sutherland, A., 'A Model of the ERM crisis', CEPR Discussion Paper No.879 (1994)

Ozkan, F.G. and Sutherland, A., 'Policy Measures to Avoid a Currency Crisis,' Economic Journal vol. 105 (1995) 510-19

Padoa-Schioppa, T., 'The September storm: EMS and the future of EMU', International Economic Outlook, vol.2 no.2 (1992) 4-8.

Portes, Richard, 'EMS and EMU After the Fall', The World Economy, vol.16 no.1 (1993) 1-16.

Roberts, Richard, '"A Tremendous Panic": The Global Financial Crisis of 1914', in Smith, Andrew, Mollan, Simon, and Tennent, Kevin D., *The Impact of the First World War on International Business* (London: Routledge, 2017)

Smith, Andrew, Mollan, Simon, and Tennent, Kevin D., *The Impact of the First World War on International Business* (Abingdon: Routledge, 2017)

Solomon, Robert, *The International Monetary System 1945-1976* (New York: Harpers & Row, 1977)

Soros, George, *Soros on Soros: Staying Ahead of the Curve* (Chichester: Wiley, 1995)

Soros, George, *The Crisis of Global Capitalism* (New York: Public Affairs, 1998)

Sotiropoulos, Dimitris P. 'Revisiting the 1992-93 EMS Crisis in the Context of International Political Economy', Kingston University London Economics Discussion Paper 2012-7 (October 2012)

Stephens, Philip, *Politics and the Pound: The Tories, the Economy and Europe* (Basingstoke: Macmillan, 1997)

Stevens, Glenn, 'The Asian Crisis: A Retrospective', Bulletin of the Reserve Bank of Australia (August 2007)

Stiglitz, Joseph E., *The Euro and Its Threat to the Future of Europe* (London: Allen Lane, 2016)

Szász, André, *The Road to Monetary Union* (Basingstoke: Palgrave Macmillan, 1999)

Thatcher, Margaret, *The Downing Street Years* (London: Harper, 1993)

Tietmeyer, Hans, *Herausforderung Euro* (Munich: Carl Hanser, 2005)

Tsoukalis, Lokas, *The Politics and Economics of European Monetary Integration* (London: George Allen & Unwin, 1977)

Wall, Stephen, *A Stranger in Europe* (Oxford: Oxford University Press, 2008)

Walsh, James I., *European Monetary Integration & Domestic Politics: Britain, France, and Italy* (London: Lynne Rienner, 2000)

Young, Hugo, *This Blessed Plot: Britain and Europe from Churchill to Blair* (Basingstoke: Macmillan, 2016)

DRAMATIS PERSONAE

Alphandéry, Edmond (1943-) Minister of Economy (France) (1993-95), Mayor of Longué-Jumelles (1977-2008)

Amato, Giuliano (1938-) Prime Minister of Italy (1992-93; 2000-01), Minister of Treasury (1987-89), Minister of the Interior (2006-08)

Andreotti, Giulio (1919-2013) Prime Minister of Italy (1976-73; 1976-79; 1989-92)

Baker, James (1930-) Secretary of the Treasury (US) (1985-88), Secretary of State (US) (1989-92)

Baker, Kenneth (1934-) Conservative Party Chairman (UK) (1989-90)

Balladur, Édouard (1929-) Minister of Finance (France) (1986-88), Prime Minister of France (1993-95)

Barucci, Piero (1933-) Minister of Treasury and Civil Service (Italy) (1992-93), Minister of Treasury (Italy) (1993-94)

Bérégovoy, Pierre (1925-93) Minister of Economy and Finance (France) (1984-86, 1988-92), Prime Minister (1992-93)

Bitterlich, Joachim (1948-) Adviser to Chancellor for European Policy (1987-93), Permanent Representative of Germany to the North Atlantic Treaty Organisation (1998-99), German Ambassador to Spain (1999-2002)

Blessing, Karl (1900-71) President, Deutsche Bundesbank (1958-69)

Brady, Nicholas (1930-) Secretary of the Treasury (US) (1988-93)

Brandt, Willy (1913-92) Chancellor of West Germany (1969-74)

Brown, Gordon (1951-) Chancellor of the Exchequer (1997-2007), Prime Minister of the UK (2007-10)

Budd, Alan (1937-) Chief Economic Adviser, Treasury (UK) (1991-97)

Burns, Terence (1944-) Permanent Secretary, Treasury (UK) (1991-98), President, National Institute of Economic and Social Research (2003-10)

Callaghan, James (1912-2005) Chancellor of the Exchequer (1964-67), Prime Minister of the UK (1976-79)

Camdessus, Michel (1933-) Governor, Banque de France (1984-87), Managing Director, International Monetary Fund (1987-2000),

Cameron, David (1966-) Special Adviser to the Chancellor of the Exchequer (1992-93), Leader of the Opposition (2005-10), Prime Minister (2010-16)

Carli, Guido (1914-93) Governor, Banca d'Italia (1960-75)

Chirac, Jacques (1932-) Prime Minister of France (1974-76; 1986-88), President (1995-2007)

Ciampi, Carlo (1920-2016) Governor, Banca d'Italia (1979-93), Prime Minister of Italy (1993-94), President (1999-2006)

Clarke, Kenneth (1940-) Home Secretary (1992-93), Chancellor of the Exchequer (1993-97)

Coleby, Anthony (1936-) Director for Monetary Affairs, Bank of England (1990-94)

Crockett, Andrew (1943-2012) Director for International Affairs, Bank of England (1989-93), General Manager, Bank for International Settlements (1994-2003)

Delors, Jacques (1925-) Minister of Finance (France) (1981-84), President, European Commission (1985-95)

Dini, Lamberto (1931-) Director General, Banca d'Italia (1979-94)

Draghi, Mario (1947-) Director General, Italian Treasury (1991-2001), Governor, Banca d'Italia (2005-11), President, European Central Bank (2011-)

Druckenmiller, Stanley (1953-) Lead Portfolio Manager, Quantum Fund (1988-2000)

Duisenberg, Wim (1935-2005) President, Nederlandsche Bank (1982-97), President, European Central Bank (1998-2003)

Emminger, Otmar (1911-86) Deputy President, Deutsche Bundesbank (1970-77), President (1977-79)

de Gaulle, Charles (1890-1970) President of France (1959-69)

Genscher, Hans-Dietrich (1927-2016) Foreign Minister (Germany) (1974-92)

George, Edward 'Eddie' (1938-2009) Deputy Governor, Bank of England (1990-93), Governor (1993-2003)

Giscard d'Estaing, Valéry (1926-) Minister of Finance (France) (1969-74), President (1974-81)

Healey, Denis (1917-2015) Chancellor of the Exchequer (1974-79)

Heath, Edward (1916-2005) Prime Minister of the UK (1970-74)

Heseltine, Michael (1993-) President of the Board of Trade and Secretary of State for Trade and Industry (UK) (1992-95), Deputy Prime Minister (1995-97)

Heywood, Jeremy (1961-) Principal Private Secretary to Chancellor of the Exchequer (1992-99), Principal Private Secretary to the Prime Minister (1999-2003, 2008-10,), Permanent Secretary, Downing Street (2010-11), Cabinet Secretary (2011-), Head of the Civil Service (2014-)

Howe, Geoffrey (1926-2015) Chancellor of the Exchequer (1979-83), Secretary of State for Foreign and Commonwealth Affairs (1983-89), Deputy Prime Minister (1989-90)

Hurd, Douglas (1930-) Home Secretary (1985-89), Secretary of State for Foreign and Commonwealth Affairs (1989-95)

Issing, Otmar (1936-) Chief Economist, Deutsche Bundesbank (1990-98), Chief Economist, European Central Bank (1998-2006)

Jones, Paul Tudor (1954-) Founder, Tudor Investment Corporation (1980-)

Kohl, Helmut (1930-2017) Minister-President of Rhineland-Palatinate (1969-76), Chancellor of West Germany/Germany (1982-98)

Köhler, Horst (1943-) State Secretary, Ministry of Finance (Germany) (1990-93), Managing Director, International Monetary Fund (2000-04), President of Germany (2004-10)

Kovner, Bruce (1945-) Chief Executive Officer, Caxton Associates (1983-2011)

Lagayette, Philippe (1944-) Deputy Governor, Banque de France (1984-92), Chief Executive, Caisse des dépôts et Consignations (1992-97)

Lahnstein, Manfred (1937-) Minister of Finance (1982-83) (West Germany)

Lamont, Norman (1942-) Financial Secretary to the Treasury (1986-89), Chief Secretary to the Treasury (1989-90), Chancellor of the Exchequer (1990-93)

de Larosière, Jacques (1929-) Managing Director, International Monetary Fund (1978-87), President, Banque de France (1987-93)

Lawson, Nigel (1932-) Chancellor of the Exchequer (1983-89)

Leigh-Pemberton, Robin (1926-2013) Governor, Bank of England (1983-93)

Lubbers, Ruud (1939-) Minister of Economic Affairs (Netherlands), (1973-77) Prime Minister (1982-94)

Macmillan, Harold (1894-1986) Chancellor of the Exchequer (1955-57), Prime Minister (1957-63)

Major, John (1943-) Chancellor of the Exchequer (1989-90), Prime Minister (1990-97)

Marjolin, Robert (1911-86) Secretary General, Organisation for European Economic Co-operation (1948-55), European Commissioner for Economic and Financial Affairs (1958-67)

Mitterrand, François (1916-96) First Secretary, Socialist Party (1971-81), President of France (1981-95)

Möllemann, Jürgen (1945-2003) Minister of Economics (Germany) (1991-93)

Plenderleith, Ian (1943-) Director for Markets, Bank of England (1990-94)

Pöhl, Karl Otto (1929-2014) State Secretary, Ministry of Finance (West Germany) (1972-77), Deputy President Deutsche Bundesbank (1977-80), President, (1980-91)

Pompidou, Georges (1911-74) Prime Minister of France (1962-68), President (1969-74)

Powell, Charles (1941-) Private Secretary to Prime Minister Margaret Thatcher (1984-90), Private Secretary to Prime Minister John Major (1990-91)

Sapin, Michel (1952-) Minister of Finance (France) (1992-93; 2014-17)

Schlesinger, Helmut (1924-) Deputy President, Deutsche Bundesbank (1980-91), President (1991-93)

Schmidt, Helmut (1918-2015) Chancellor of West Germany (1974-82)

Soros, George (1930-) Founder, The Quantum Fund (1969-)

Szász, André (1932-2017) Executive Director, Nederlansche Bank (1973-94)

Thatcher, Margaret (1925-2013) Prime Minister of the UK (1979-90)

Tietmeyer, Hans (1931-2016) Deputy President, Deutsche Bundesbank (1991-93), President (1993-99)

Trichet, Jean-Claude (1942-) Director of the Treasury (France) (1987-94), Governor, Banque de France (1993-2003), President, European Central Bank (2003-11)

Turnbull, Andrew (1945-) Principal Private Secretary to the Prime Minister (UK) (1988-92), Permanent Secretary to the Treasury (1998-2002), Cabinet Secretary (2002-05)

Waigel, Theo (1939-) Finance Minister (Germany) (1989-98)

Wall, Stephen (1947-) Private Secretary to the Foreign Secretary (UK) (1988-91), Private Secretary to the Prime Minister (1991-93), Permanent Representative to the EU (1995-2000), EU adviser to the Prime Minister (2000-04)

Walters, Alan (1926-2009) Economic Adviser to Prime Minister of the UK (1981-83; 1989)

Werner, Pierre (1913-2002) Prime Minister of Luxembourg (1959-74; 1979-84)

Wicks, Nigel (1940-) Principal Private Secretary to Prime Minister of the UK (1985-90), Second Permanent Secretary with responsibility for International Finance, Treasury (1988-2000), Principal Private Secretary to Prime Minister (1990-92)

INDEX

Agnelli, Gianni *16*
Alchemy of Finance, The 13
Ahern, Bertie *18*
Alphandéry, Edmond *131, 133*
Amato, Giuliano *91-93, 100, 104*

Baker, James *45*
Baker, Kenneth *55, 64*
Balladur, Edouard *47, 131-33*
Banca d'Italia *94, 99, 100, 145*
Bank of America *5, 121*
Bank of England
    arguments on monetary union *32*
    Black Wednesday trading *4, 7, 113-22*
    conversation with Schlesinger *112*
    departure from snake (1972) *33*
    discussion with Lawson, Thatcher on ERM *41, 42, 45, 46,*
    ERM entry preparations *60, 62, 68, 70-78*
    post-Black Wednesday measures, including independence *135-140, 137*
    interest rates *63-65, 67*
    lack of Bundesbank awareness *122, 150*
    lead-up to Black Wednesday *89-112*
    reserves loss *3, 10, 16, 33, 105, 111, 114-118, 120, 121, 139*
    upset over Denmark *87*
    warning on France *35*
Bank of Ireland *144*
Bank of Spain *144*
Bank of Thailand *21*
Banque de France *10, 69, 70, 87, 129-32*
Barber, Anthony *33, 42*
Barber, Lionel *110*
Barucci, Piero *103, 104*
Bérégovoy, Pierre *40, 70, 85, 88, 91, 92, 120, 128, 131*
Black Wednesday *113-135*
    effect on economic recovery in 1992-97 *9, 135, 138, 140*
    financial consequences for Treasury *4, 114*
    Franco-German aftermath *128-133, 138, 142*

    impact on the French franc *127-133*
    political and economic consequences *122, 137-51*
    setback for Lamont and Conservatives *75, 77*
    Treasury's measures *4, 114-17, 150*
Blair, Tony *141*
Blessing, Karl *29*
Bonn *38, 42, 77, 83, 87, 90, 92, 108, 120, 142*
    Bonn chancellery *100*
    Bonn 'grand coalition' government *30*
    Bundesbank-Bonn co-operation *83*
Brady, Nicolas *84*
Brandt, Willy *31, 32, 35*
Bretton Woods system *11, 17, 18, 22, 23, 27, 29, 32, 35, 38, 46*
Bretton Woods conference of 1944 *26*
Brexit *40, 113, 148, 149*
Brittan, Samuel *48*
Broughton, James *22*
Brown, Gordon *50, 136, 140, 141, 148*
Brummer, Alex *16*
Budd, Alan *108, 109, 115, 122, 139, 140*
Bundesbank
    apology to British ambassador *87*
    Bundesbank-Bonn co-operation *83*
    Bundesbank council *103, 106*
    Bundesbank-dominated ERM *149*
    Bundesbank Law *128*
    change of opinion on monetary union *142, 143*
    controversy over pressure on sterling, lira and French franc (1992) *88-94, 99-122, 127, 129, 130, 136*
    French franc crisis (1993) *131-34*
    French proposals on monetary union *29, 30*
    opt-out from the obligation to support ERM currencies *100*
    possible model for Britain *10*
    preparations for British ERM membership *41-43, 45, 49, 62, 69-72*
    rumours of British 'mole' *150*
    Schlesinger interview on 15 September 1992 *5, 8-10, 14-16*

Also by OMFIF Press

A FRANK ASSESSMENT OF TRUMP'S FIRST THREE MONTHS IN OFFICE

Written by Lord (Meghnad) Desai and fellow authors, *Trump: The First One Hundred Days* looks at the actions President Donald Trump has taken in office over his first 100 days in office and the likely effects on the US and global economic and political scenes. It includes insight into the state of the economy inherited by Trump.

'No incoming president could have asked to inherit a better economic legacy. The cost of servicing US debt as a percentage of GDP has rarely been cheaper. But the US economy is not as indestructible as Donald Trump assumes.'
Meghnad Desai, UK House of Lords; Emeritus Professor of Economics, London School of Economics and Political Science

'If Trump's policies succeed, he wins. If they fail, he can shift the blame to the establishment. As his time passes, Trump is more likely to make new enemies than new friends.'
Brian Reading, Economic Adviser, UK Prime Minister Edward Heath (1966-72)

'He still has much to learn, and can embarrass himself by his ignorance. A typical misstep came at the end of February, when he foolishly exclaimed, 'Nobody knew that healthcare could be so complicated.' Well, yes, in fact everyone did.'
Reginald Dale, Senior Fellow and Director, Transatlantic Media Network

To purchase the book visit omfif.org/shop

OMFIF

Also by OMFIF Press

LEARNING LESSONS FROM ASIA AFTER THE GLOBAL FINANCIAL CRISIS

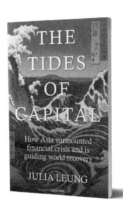

In *The Tides of Capital: How Asia surmounted the financial crisis and is guiding world recovery* Julia Leung distils two decades of financial diplomacy into an incisive account of the lessons Asia and the world have learned from successive bouts of crisis management. She entreats the West to take seriously Asia's growing clout on the world economic stage.

'Julia Leung has written a wonderful, highly readable, short book on international capital flows, on mistakes made and lessons learned in Asia on the management of the capital account, in and out of crisis mode.'
Prof. Michael Spence, recipient, 2001 Nobel Memorial Prize in Economic Sciences; New York University

'Even in this crowded field, this is a most welcome contribution. As we seek to build a global financial system for the future, Leung's recommendations on the pragmatic use of a diverse set of policies by Asian governments are worth serious study.'
Dr Victor Fung, Chairman, Fung Global Institute

'Julia Leung pulls no punches in describing the shortcomings in US and European economic policy that resulted in the global financial crisis. She presents Asia's more eclectic and pragmatic approach as the way forward.'
Prof. Barry Eichengreen, University of California, Berkeley

To purchase the book visit omfif.org/shop

OMFIF

Also by OMFIF Press

A COMPELLING TALE OF AFRICA'S NEW WORLD ROLE AT THE CROSSROADS OF GLOBAL CAPITAL

The Convergence of Nations: Why Africa's time is now is a compilation of international analysis and opinion on Africa's political, economic and social realities. Jean-Claude Bastos de Morais leads a team of 31 authors illuminating Africa's opportunities and emphasising Africa's massive potential for profiting from globalisation.

'As always, Africa must aim high. This is a compellingly realistic summary of all the big themes affecting Africa's future, and I warmly commend it.'
Akinwumi Adesina, President, African Development Bank

'Africa's inclusive socio-economic transformation requires convergence of international ideas, initiatives, resources and shared vision. The book provides an invaluable new vista for the continent's future prosperity. I commend it highly.'
Linah K. Mohohlo, Governor, Bank of Botswana

'At a time when risks elsewhere have been growing, this book spells out how Africa could be a winner. The precondition is that the continent tackles its problems of corruption, weak governance and misallocation of resources.'
Jacques de Larosière, Managing Director of the IMF (1978-87)

To purchase the book visit omfif.org/shop

OMFIF

Also by OMFIF Press

THE 1976 SAGA REVISTED
BRITAIN'S IMF CRISIS 40 YEARS ON

The 1976 IMF crisis was a time of upheaval in Britain's post-war economic fortunes. As the UK could no longer cover its financial deficits, there was no choice but to turn to the IMF to avoid extreme economic pain and even default. Richard Roberts' account unveils the intricacies of a watershed in British and international economic history.

'This book is remarkable. Was the Labour government response to the crisis a 'breakthrough' marking the departure from Keynes' policies? The lasting lesson, still valid today, is that floating down one's currency is never a lasting solution.'
Jacques de Larosière, Managing Director of the IMF (1978-87)

'This was a new dimension of sterling crisis: a balance of payments crisis combined with Labour government tension and a trial of strength with the IMF. Roberts explains the mainsprings of the upheavals in this profound book.'
Prof. Helmut Schlesinger, President, Deutsche Bundesbank (1991-93)

'This book makes for fascinating reading. Covering unemployment, inflation and balooning deficits, these are issues that remain with us - lessons to be learned.'
Nout Wellink, President, Nederlandsche Bank (1997-2011)

To purchase the book visit omfif.org/shop

OMFIF

OMFIF Analysis

The *Global Public Investor 2017* is the fourth of OMFIF's annual reports devoted to public sector asset ownership and management across a range of official institutions around the world. Global Public Investors encompass many different types of institutions, including central banks, sovereign funds and public pension funds, linked by their status as public sector-funded entities and representing a core component of world capital markets, with total holdings estimated at $33.8tn.

'The need for improved and sustainable developments is increasing, and financing these adds pressure on mainstream lenders. Global Public Investors must play an active role in meeting this challenge.'
Thierry de Longuemar, Asian Infrastructure Investment Bank

'Global Public Investor 2017 is the fourth in the OMFIF series of annual reports that document the emergence of a powerful investor class around the world – public institutions that are stewards of national savings in various forms.'
Dennis Lockhart, formerly Federal Reserve Bank of Atlanta

'We are delighted to support OMFIF's prestigious publication, and believe that it will help enhance our understanding of the opportunities and challenges facing Global Public Investors in Asia and the Lusophone world.'
Anselmo Teng, Monetary Authority of Macau

To purchase the book visit omfif.org/shop

By the same authors

William Keegan
Consulting Father Wintergreen (1974)
A Real Killing (1976)
Who Runs the Economy? (with Rupert Pennant-Rea) (1978)
Mrs Thatcher's Economic Experiment (1984)
Britain Without Oil (1985)
Mr Lawson's Gamble (1989)
The Spectre of Capitalism (1992)
2066 and All That (2000)
The Prudence of Mr Gordon Brown (2004)
Saving the World? – Gordon Brown Reconsidered (2012)
Mr Osborne's Economic Experiment (2014)

David Marsh
Germany – Rich, Bothered and Divided (1989),
re-released in 1990 as *The New Germany*
The Bundesbank – The Bank that Rules Europe (1992)
Germany and Europe – The Crisis of Unity (1994)
The Euro – The Politics of the New Global Currency (2009), re-released in 2011
as *The Battle for the New Global Currency*
Europe's Deadlock: How the Crisis Could Be Solved – And Why It Won't Happen
(2013), re-released in 2016 as *Europe's Deadlock: How the Crisis Could Be Solved
– And Why It Still Won't Happen*

Richard Roberts
Schroders: Merchants and Bankers (1992)
Inside International Finance (1998)
*Take Your Partners: Orion, the Consortium Banks and the Transformation of
the Euromarkets* (2001)
*City State: A Contemporary History of the City of London and How Money
Triumphed* (2002) *(with David Kynaston)*
Wall Street (2003)
The City (2008)
*Did Anyone Learn Anything from Equitable Life? Lessons and Learning from
Financial Crises* (2012)
Saving the City: The Great Financial Crisis of 1914 (2013)
The Lion Wakes: A Modern History of HSBC (with David Kynaston) (2015)
When Britain went Bust: The 1976 IMF Crisis (2016)